· NOTHIN' BUT THE BEST ·
· ITALIAN-AMERICAN CLASSICS ·
· FROM OUR BLOCK TO YOURS ·

STATEN ITALY

FRANCIS GARCIA AND SAL BASILLE

Founders of ARTICHOKE PIZZA

with Rachel Holtzman

GRAND CENTRAL
Life & Style
NEW YORK · BOSTON

Grand Central Life & Style
Hachette Book Group
1290 Avenue of the Americas
New York, NY 10104

www.GrandCentralLifeandStyle.com

Printed in the United States of America

Design by Gary Tooth/ Empire Design Studio

Q-MA

First Edition: April 2015

10 9 8 7 6 5 4 3 2 1

Grand Central Life & Style is an imprint of Grand Central Publishing.

The Grand Central Life & Style name and logo are trademarks of Hachette Book Group, Inc.

The Hachette Speakers Bureau provides a wide range of authors for speaking events. To find out more, go to www.HachetteSpeakersBureau.com or call (866) 376-6591.

The publisher is not responsible for websites (or their content) that are not owned by the publisher.

Library of Congress Cataloging-in-Publication Data

Garcia, Francis (Restaurateur)

  Staten Italy : nothin' but the best Italian-American classics, from our block to yours / Francis Garcia and Sal Basille, the founders of Artichoke Pizza ; with Rachel Holtzman. — First edition.

      pages cm

  Includes index.

  ISBN 978-1-4555-8354-6 (hardcover) — ISBN 978-1-4555-8353-9 (ebook)
 1. Cooking, Italian.   2. Cooking—New York.   I. Basille, Sal.   II. Holtzman, Rachel.   III. Title.

  TX723.G255 2015

  641.5945—dc23

                                                      2014035838

Dedicated with love to Joy Garcia (right) and Bella Basille (center), our mothers.

Ma—without youse, New York would starve.

CONTENTS

— WELCOME TO —

STATEN ITALY

Five years ago, when we told our family that we were leaving behind four generations of restaurant business in Staten Island and Brooklyn to open our own shop in Manhattan, Fran's mother said to us: "They're gonna chew you up and spit you out." She told us that we were gonna lose all our money, that we had no idea what we were doing, and that there was a pizzeria on every corner in the city.

But we did it anyway. We borrowed the cash, we built it ourselves, and we stuck to what we knew—pizza and beer. After being open for just a few weeks, there was already a line around the corner. People would ask who our publicist was, and all we'd say was, "What's a publicist?" We were doing what we did best and what we loved to do: feedin' people and feedin' 'em well.

Then we started cooking other food besides pizza. Francis would bring in a couple of heads of cauliflower, mix 'em with some cheese, eggs, and parsley, fry 'em up into little pancakes on an electric griddle, and put 'em out on the counter. People were flippin' out for them too. They'd sell out as soon as they came outta the fryer. So we started doing the same thing with Aunt Loulou's Escarole Fritters, Grandma's Meatballs, Stuffed Artichokes, and Fried Rice Balls.

This wasn't the food that you see on fancy Italian menus, and it sure wasn't the stuff they eat in Italy. We might have Italian roots, but we've never even been to Italy (except that one time). The only Italian words we know are the bad ones from when our grandfather would yell at us. We're Italian *American*, and this was the food we grew up eating in our homes in Staten Island—or as we like to call it, "Staten Italy."

You know the place—that little island off the boot of Manhattan where you can't swing a cannoli without hittin' an Italian. It's that special part of the world where one side of the street is your motha's brotha's sister-in-law and your fourteen cousins and the other is your best friend Joey and *his* fourteen cousins. It's where your mother or grandmother is out hollerin' at six p.m. every night for you to come in for suppa. Dinner is always an event, a production. It's never about grabbin' something quick because food is a big deal here, nothin' but the best. Sitting down to eat all together is like going to church—the most important thing on that particular day. The house smells like sizzling garlic and oil—because Grandma always says she can make anything taste good with garlic and oil—and on the table are things like Broccoli Rabe and Sausage, Lucky Clams with Parsley and Garlic, Pork Cutlets with Vinegar Peppers, Chicken Rollatini, and Broiled Legs and Thighs with Lemon.

Whether you're Italian or not, this is the kind of food we all grew up eating. It's the ultimate comfort food. It's why people line up around the block to eat at our six restaurants, and it's definitely why two cousins from Staten Island could go from peeling garlic in their mothers' shop to having a hit show on the Cooking Channel. It's a hot, steaming bowl of Mussels Marinara with Linguine, served up with a side of nostalgia. Okay, so maybe your mother was doling out peanut butter and jelly and chicken à la king, but when you went out to eat? We're willing to bet that your favorite meals were the ones you ate at that old-school Italian joint—the one with the heaping plates of pasta smothered with red sauce and topped with fistfuls of grated cheese.

....

This book is our way of sharing a little slice of Staten Island with the rest of the world. It's the recipes and traditions that have been handed down through four generations of our family, recipes as full of Italian-American flavor and personality as the kitchens in Red Hook and Carroll Gardens and Staten Island where they were originally made. This is definitely not some kind of wannabe-authentic Red Sauce situation written by a couple of guys who are classically trained in some foo-foo cuisine. For us, this is what was on our table growing up, plain and simple, and it's what we now serve for a living. It's the fish suppers that were always on Friday; the beans and macaroni that were on the table two, three days a week; the Sunday gravy that was cooked up with neck bones, short ribs, and braciole that was outta this world. It's the huge pots of crab sauce our grandpa Dominick cooked down at the docks, the sandshark that everybody else was throwing back in the water but that we grilled up with a red wine gravy, the gigantic icebox cakes Aunt Loulou always made, and the roast beef our grandma drilled a hole through so she could stuff it full of garlic and parsley. It was the meatballs we ate with Italian bread on Sunday, and

Clockwise from top left: Grandma Connie and Grandpa Dominick in their hero shop; Basille's on Forest Avenue in Staten Island; Dolly with Sal's father, Vito, and Aunt Loulou; Artichoke Pizza on 14th Street; Grandma Connie with Sal's father, Vito, and Uncle Mikey; Diners at Basille's in Staten Island then ate again on Wonder Bread for lunch on Monday. And it's definitely the cold eggplant. Because no matter what was being cooked or what we were celebrating—Easter, Christmas, Lent, your birthday, Tuesday—that eggplant was always on the friggin' table.

These recipes are our childhood memories. Every time we eat these things, it takes us back to when Frank Sinatra or Tony Bennett was on the radio, and we kids would be waitin' in the dining room for the adults to bring out dinner, or hanging around in the kitchen, eating Cauliflower Fritters right outta the pan. Our grandpa Dominick would be manning that macaroni pot, taking it so serious, always asking, "Should I turn the water on yet? Should I put the salt in yet?" He'd be making five, six pounds of spaghetti because everybody in our family cooked for an army. We didn't know how to cook for two people. When our grandpa made a sandwich, he used the whole loaf of bread. Thing was, he loved feedin' people. And if there's one thing that we got from him, it's that. In the eighties, he owned a hero shop on Clinton Street in Red Hook, Brooklyn. Every Sunday after cooking us a huge meal, he'd go for a few hours and feed the homeless. Because that's what he loved to do. Even the pigeons around his shop were too fat to fly—true story. He'd feed them all his leftover bread, and we swear those pigeons got to be the largest birds you've ever seen in your life. As he got older and had more time on his hands, he cooked even more. He started jarring tomatoes, pickling eggplant, and makin' bread crumbs. It got to the point where Sal's parents' enormous three-car garage was packed to the fenders with all this stuff. When Grandpa was around, you weren't leaving his presence without a jar of eggplant or tomatoes or something. And after he was gone, we were still eating his eggplant five, six years later. We'd put some vinegar and oil on it and have it with some Italian bread and cheese and olives. It was his legacy to us.

For us, it's always been about food. When we were rewarded, it was with food. When we were bad, we got no food. Or sometimes we got even better food because we got a beatin' and then our parents would feel guilty. It's in our family's blood, all this food. After arriving on Ellis Island at the turn of the century, our great-grandfather opened the Mona Lisa pastry shop down on Court Street in Brooklyn. In the fifties, our grandparents opened their first little sandwich shop. Grandpa Dominick ran the place while also working as a longshoreman down at the piers. But he went into the hero business full-time when the shop got so popular that our uncles opened four more within a two-mile radius.

Eventually, our mothers opened a few restaurants on their own with their husbands, and in 1995, came together to run Basille's down on Forest Avenue in Staten Island. It seated 110 people—160 in the summer—and served New York–style pizza and home-style Italian-American dishes made with good ingredients, fresh sauces, and generations of experience. It was the kinda place where you knew all the customers by name, and they'd be bringing in pictures of their kids and their new babies and whatnot. Our grandparents would open in the daytime, peel the eggplant, roll the meatballs, season the bread crumbs, cook all the sauce; and then Sal's mom, Bella, would come in at night to work the line. Fran's mom waitressed, and we would bounce between doing our homework in the apartment upstairs and doing all the jobs the grown-ups didn't want to do. In the restaurant business you gotta start somewhere—either by peelin' garlic or openin' clams. We always got the openin' clams job, so by the time we were twelve, we could snap open clams so fast, forgettaboutit. We'd help slice onions, grind tomatoes for sauce, and bus tables. When we wanted to start our own shop, the food business was runnin' through our veins too.

Now we're sharing these family traditions with you. It's our way of saying, "Try this, eat that, sample these," the way our grandpa Dominick was always doin'. There's nothing fancy about this food. But when you put it all together, these recipes make some of the most delicious things you eva ate. And that just feels like our home. So pull up a chair and pour a glass of Dewar's, because you don't know what you've been missin'.

—*Francis "Fran" Garcia and Sal "Sally" Basille*

Great-Aunt Tessie and Grandma Connie

1

GET THE GROCERIES

STOCKING THE KITCHEN AND GEARING UP

OUTTA THE TRUNK

Yⲟu don't need anything fancy to make the food our family made, but you do need a few good basic ingredients and pieces of equipment. Here are our recommendations.

PANTRY

SALT: MORTON TABLE SALT. The girl with the umbrella. Some salt isn't as salty as other salt because of the iodization process, and this is the saltiest one. When we make our dough over at Artichoke, we always use Morton's. Sysco tried sellin' us a cheaper salt, but it just wasn't as good. We know it's fashionable to cook with sea salt and kosher salt and stuff like that, and maybe it's healthier. But for our recipes, it's mostly Morton's.

OLIVE OIL: FILIPPO BERIO. It's the one we know and the one we like, but you could go with any other brand that tastes good to you. Just look for one that doesn't say "extra virgin." It's important to know the difference between the types of olive oil available, because it really affects the flavor. The very first press of the olives is extra virgin, the second is virgin, and the third is what's called pomace. That's the one you're lookin' for—one that doesn't say "extra virgin" or "virgin" on the label, just "olive oil." It doesn't have the strong, almost bitter flavor of extra virgin, which can get in the way of a dish. If you fry something in extra-virgin olive oil or use it to make a sauce, that's all you're gonna taste. Plus, it's expensive.

You can buy a gallon of pomace for like ten bucks. Save the extra-virgin stuff for things like dressin' a salad or dippin' bread. All the recipes in this book are made using pomace unless otherwise noted.

BUTTER: BREAKSTONE'S. All the way. And always salted. It's what we had growin' up, and to this day, if there's toast, it's got Breakstone's on it. We like the way it tastes and we like the way it melts. All the recipes in this book call for salted butter unless otherwise noted.

PASTA: RONZONI. It's what we've always bought and what we're used to. Though frankly, as far as dried pasta goes, it's just about the same from brand to brand. It's pretty much all packed in the same place. As for dry versus fresh, we personally prefer dry pasta. It's not as doughy, and you can keep it in the cabinet for five years—it'll never go bad. Having said that, you gotta go fresh for tortellini and ravioli because of the fillings. We use Pastosa, a Staten Island institution that distributes around the country. We're not just fans because they're locals—we've yet to find a better fresh pasta.

TOMATOES: REDPACK AND TUTTOROSSO. These are the best, and it doesn't hurt that our good friend's father owns the company. Don't be fooled by all the San Marzano nonsense. San Marzano is a region of Italy that supposedly has the best soil and weather for growin' tomatoes. But our friend's father will tell you that it's a load of bull. A lotta these companies are just buyin' tomatoes in California and passin' 'em off as San Marzano. So the way to find the best tomatoes is to go with the ones that taste the best to you, whether they're from Italy, California, or New Jersey.

GOOD ITALIAN BREAD: Look for one that's crusty on the outside, not soft. It'll stay good for two days, tops. Eat it fresh on day one, butter and toast it the next, then turn it into bread crumbs or Italian French Toast (page 39) after that.

PECORINO AND PARMIGIANO-REGGIANO: The two heavyweight champions of cheese. And we use Pecorino Romano, but any pecorino is good. We recommend buying your cheese in hunks, ungrated. But if you'd rather buy it grated, you don't want the Kraft product that looks like a can of Ajax. You want one that's in the deli section, ideally grated that day.

THE REST:

- All-purpose flour
- Anchovies
- Black pepper (pre-ground is okay)
- Bouillon cubes
- Bread crumbs (see our recipes on pages 79 and 82)
- Canned beans (cannellini and chickpea)
- Chicken stock
- Dried parsley
- Garlic
- Onions
- Oscar Mayer bacon
- Red pepper flakes
- Rice
- Tomato paste
- Tomato puree

EQUIPMENT

NICE, BIG POT—Make that two, so you can be makin' sauce in one and boilin' macaroni in the other. They've gotta be a good, heavy gauge, especially for when you're cookin' sauce for hours. If it's a cheap pot, you're gonna burn the sauce.

FRYIN' PANS—The kind you smack somebody in the head with. You want 'em nice and heavy, like cast iron or stainless steel. Heavy metal absorbs and distributes the heat more evenly, like the way a pizza oven works. With a cheap pan, you only get hot spots where the heat is hittin' the pan. When you're fryin' meatballs or cauliflower fritters, you don't want to have to be moving things around to get into those hot spots.

GOOD CHOPPIN' KNIFE— One with a little bit of weight to it.

TONGS—You gotta have tongs. Use 'em to turn things in the oven and on the grill, flip things that are fryin', you name it.

CUTTING BOARD—For choppin' garlic and onions.

STRAINER—Or as we called it, a *scolapasta*, pronounced "scool-bas." It was one of the few Italian words we used in the house.

WOODEN SPOON—Especially for stirrin' the sauce. A metal spoon leaves a metal taste.

BOWLS—For mixin' and servin'.

CHEESE GRATER—And don't forget to put it out on the table.

THE REST:

Food processor—to make life easy

Pizza stone or tiles (see pages 120–23)

Wooden board for servin' cheese

Baskets for servin' Italian bread

Rags or kitchen towels—for dryin' your hands, cleanin' up spills, and using as oven mitts

Aprons

Grandpa Dominick and Grandma
Connie at breakfast

2

— THE BEST PART OF WAKIN' UP —

BREAKFAST

reakfast was like any other meal in our houses—very serious business. There were easily fifteen to twenty of us at the table, between our families and all the friends and girlfriends and boyfriends that were always sleepin' over. A lot of times we'd end up at Sal's, where our grandparents were living. They'd wake us up in the morning by ringin' a bell from the basement or bangin' a fork on a plate. We'd all go downstairs and it'd be like a diner, with our grandfather workin' the line in his Continental slacks, white Fruit of the Loom tank top, and big gold chain with a big gold anchor hanging from it (not to mention the glasses with lenses like the bottoms of old-fashioned Coke bottles): "You want eggs? You want French toast? Waddya want?" He'd get up at four a.m. just to start cooking, and by the time we were all eatin' breakfast, he'd be sitting down to a bowl of macaroni for lunch.

On the table there'd be a big pot of melted butter and doughnuts—because no matter how huge breakfast was, somebody would always go out and get the doughnuts. They were like the eggplant of breakfast. If Uncle Greg was over, you could bet Court Street pastry would be there. If it was the weekend, there were bagels. *Always* bagels. Also, fresh eggs from the backyard. Sal's father used to say, "You want eggs? Get 'em yourself." We still remember going out to the coop barefoot in the wet grass and gathering the eggs in a basket. They'd still be warm, they were so fresh. Covered in turds, but fresh.

Since we were usually heading out to school, the food was easy to make—sauce and eggs, mortadella and eggs, potatoes and eggs, peppers and eggs. See where we're going here? Our grandfather's hero shop made a business outta those kinds of dishes. He used to write 'em up on a chalkboard and it was all, "Potatoes and Eggs," "Peppers and Eggs," and "Eggs and Potatoes." One time a guy came in and asked, "What's the difference between Potatoes and Eggs and Eggs and Potatoes?"

Our grandfather responded, "Nothin'."

"So why did you write it twice?" the guy says.

"Because I needed to fill the board."

They were all different variations on the same thing, but they were always delicious. And all you had to do was throw everything in a pan for the kind of gut-bustin', satisfying meal that the truckers and factory workers and long-shoremen from the piers would go nuts for.

If it was Saturday or Sunday, by the time we cleared the breakfast table we were already getting ready for dinner, makin' the sauce, rollin' the meatballs. But if it was during the week, our grandfather would be taking everyone's orders for when we got home—baked ziti, chicken cutlets, you name it. "Who's comin' ova?" That was always the question. You can bet we made a lot of friends that way.

> ### A NOTE ON OUR SERVING SIZES
>
> While we did our best to give you an idea of how many people our recipes serve, we don't exactly eat like regular humans. What might suit six regular people from Connecticut might feed one *gavone* from the block. We'd say we're sorry for givin' you too many leftovers, but chances are you'll be thankin' us for the favor.

POTATOES AND EGGS

SERVES 3 TO 6

Growing up, we ate this all the time, and not only for breakfast. If Fran's mother was working late or there wasn't a lot of time for dinner, she'd make a gigantic pot of potatoes and eggs and we'd eat it up with ketchup on Italian bread. But if our grandmother was cooking this, she'd make it into a pie, almost like a quiche. Then she'd season the living daylights out of it with salt and pepper and slice it like a pizza. It's so good that we still make it that way at Solo Bella—and still eat it for breakfast, lunch, or dinner.

6 medium to large potatoes, peeled

6 medium to large onions

12 large eggs

2 teaspoons salt

2 teaspoons black pepper

1 to 1½ cups olive oil

1 loaf of bread from your favorite Italian bakery

Ketchup, for serving

Hot sauce, for serving (optional)

Cut the potatoes in half, and then cut them in half again. Now cut all those pieces in half. Then do it again. (You should have roughly 1-inch pieces now.) Set the potatoes in a dish-towel and wrap it around them like a little cradle. Give it a shake and rub the potatoes gently with the towel so it absorbs their moisture. Set them aside, still wrapped in the towel.

Cut the onions in half, then cut them in half again. Now cut those halves into 1-inch slices.

In a large bowl, beat the eggs with a whisk. Add the salt and pepper and set aside.

Heat the olive oil in a large frying pan over medium-high heat. When the oil is hot or starts to dance a little, add the potatoes. Cover the pan with a lid and let the potatoes cook for 4 to 6 minutes. Uncover the pan, turn the potatoes, cover again, and cook for 4 minutes more, or until the potatoes have begun to soften and brown.

Add the onions and cover. Cook for 5 minutes, or until the onions are soft.

Add the beaten eggs to the pan and reduce the heat to very low. (You want the heat to be very low; otherwise, you'll burn the eggs.) Cover the pan with a lid or a large plate and cook the eggs until they're cooked through but still slightly runny, 2 to 3 minutes. Remove the pan from the heat, and holding the lid or plate in place, flip the whole thing over. Slide the egg and potato mixture onto the lid or plate, then put it back into the pan so the side that was once on the bottom is now on top. Cover and cook for another minute or two.

Slice it like a pie, serve on bread as a sandwich, or pile it on a plate with ketchup and/or hot sauce on the side.

MORTADELLA AND EGGS

SERVES 1 TO 3

Mortadella—or mortadell, *as it's called in our house—is basically Italian bologna. It's a cold cut that you can find at almost any deli, and we always had some in the fridge. It fries up really nice. Fran's mom would brown it in a pan, then add butter, eggs, and Muenster cheese, and scramble it up. You could eat it just like that, or butter some bread and make a fast sandwich. The grease from the mortadella and the butter means you don't need any extra condiments, just a big glass of Tropicana OJ.*

6 large eggs, plus 1 for good measure

½ teaspoon salt

½ teaspoon black pepper

1 teaspoon chopped fresh flat-leaf parsley

¼ pound mortadella, sliced like bologna

4 tablespoons (½ stick) salted butter

4 slices Muenster cheese, torn into pieces

1 loaf of bread from your favorite Italian bakery

In a large bowl, beat the eggs with a whisk. Season with the salt, pepper, and parsley. Set aside.

Heat a large cast-iron frying pan or nonstick skillet over medium heat, then add the mortadella and let it brown. Turn the heat down to low and add 2 tablespoons of the butter.

Pour the eggs into the pan and fold in the cheese. Cook the eggs, turning them continuously with a fork or spatula, until they're fluffy and scrambled but still a little soft, 3 to 4 minutes. Remove the pan from the heat.

Slather some bread with the remaining 2 tablespoons butter, top it with the eggs and mortadella, and cut the sandwich into thirds. Go for the middle piece—always the best— and let the butter drip down your arm.

EGGS PIZZAIOLA

SERVES 1 TO 3

This is just a little somethin' that we cook up at Chubby Mary's. When you're simmering eggs in tomato gravy with garlic and oil and topping 'em with Parmigiano-Reggiano and pecorino, you're gonna end up with a totally different texture than a regular poached egg would have. You'd think you were eating the best raviolis you eva ate! You can serve 'em up right in the frying pan or slice up some Italian bread and turn the whole thing into a hero. Either way, these guys are perfect for brunch. Just don't wear white when you're makin' 'em.

3 tablespoons olive oil, plus more for serving

4 garlic cloves, chopped

½ teaspoon salt

⅛ teaspoon black pepper

½ teaspoon red pepper flakes

1 tablespoon chopped fresh flat-leaf parsley

Splash of white wine

1 (15-ounce) can Redpack crushed tomatoes

4 fresh basil leaves

6 large eggs

4 tablespoons shredded Parmigiano-Reggiano

2 tablespoons grated pecorino

Preheat the oven to 400°F.

In a medium frying pan, heat the olive oil over medium heat. Add the garlic and sauté until just golden brown. Add the salt, black pepper, red pepper flakes, parsley, and wine and let cook for about 30 seconds. Throw in the tomatoes, bring to a rapid boil, then reduce the heat to maintain a simmer. Tear up the basil, add it to the sauce, and cook gently for 7 to 10 minutes. Remove from the heat and let stand for 10 minutes. Crack the eggs directly into the sauce—taking care not to break any of the yolks—and cover with sauce so the eggs are completely submerged. Top with 2 tablespoons of the Parmigiano-Reggiano and 1 tablespoon of the pecorino.

Put the entire thing in the oven and bake for 10 to 15 minutes, or until the eggs are thoroughly cooked and no longer runny. Finish it off with the rest of the cheeses and a drizzle of olive oil and serve it directly from the frying pan.

ONIONS, PEPPERS, AND EGGS BREAKFAST HERO

SERVES 2 TO 3

This is the fastest of all the breakfast dishes that we make—even faster than Potatoes and Eggs (page 23)—because the peppers and onions cook so quickly. And yet these peppers are so delicious that you could easily eat them alone and not miss the eggs.

This also makes a great lunch. If our grandfather was packing up sandwiches for the boat and there weren't any leftovers like meatballs or eggplant, he'd make these. But really, they're great anytime, any day, particularly over episodes of I Love Lucy.

2 bell peppers, 1 green and 1 red

½ large Spanish onion

7 large eggs

1 teaspoon salt

1 teaspoon black pepper

3 tablespoons olive oil

4 tablespoons (½ stick) salted butter

1 loaf of bread from your favorite Italian bakery

Cut the bell peppers in half, remove the seeds and stems, then cut them lengthwise into 1½-inch strips. Cut the onion into ½-inch slices. Set aside.

In a large bowl, beat the eggs with a whisk and season with half the salt and black pepper. Set aside.

In a large frying pan, heat the olive oil until it starts to dance. Add the peppers and onion along with the remaining salt and black pepper. Cook until the onion is browned and the peppers are tender, about 5 minutes. The whole house should smell like peppers and onions.

Turn the heat down to medium and add 2 tablespoons of the butter and the beaten eggs. Cook the eggs, turning them continuously with a fork or spatula, until they're fluffy and scrambled but still a little soft, 3 to 4 minutes. Remove from the heat.

Slather the bread with the remaining 2 tablespoons butter, top it with the eggs and peppers, and cut it into thirds. Don't share with anybody.

Aunt Josie, Uncle Freddie, Grandma Connie, and Grandpa Dominick

W e don't know what it was with the women in our family, but they drank coffee all day. From about 7 in the morning to 5 or 6 at night—or later, if we had company—our grandmother and our moms would be drinkin' cups of coffee. It would either be Chock full o'Nuts—the best coffee you can buy in a can—or Eight O'Clock French Roast, which you could only buy at the A&P on Hylan Boulevard. They had a machine by the cashiers that would grind the beans for you; all you had to do was pour in the beans, hit a little button, and the ground coffee would fall into your bag. Our grandmother loved it.

Anyways, if they were havin' coffee, then they were also eating buttered Uneeda Biscuits. There was always a tub of Breakstone's salted, whipped butter—it had to be the tub, never the sticks—out on the table so it would be nice and soft. Our grandmother or our mothers would sit down, butter the biscuits (or Ritz Crackers, which is what Fran's mother prefers, or Social Tea Biscuits, which is what her friend Roseanne would always bring over), and dip them into the coffee. You gotta take seven or eight of them, press 'em together, and then dunk 'em. It's very nice. Or sometimes Grandma would just crumble them up and put them right in her coffee. But you don't have to be doin' it all day long for it to be a great snack or a light breakfast when you're not feelin' like cooking for an army.

SAUCE AND EGGS

SERVES 2

This is just like Eggs Pizzaiola (page 27), but unlike that dish, where the eggs cook like raviolis, here you whip 'em up into leftover gravy. Much easier. You might look in your pan and say, "Yeah, that looks like eggs," but when they get incorporated into the sauce they really become something else entirely, all fluffy and delicious. The tomatoes cook into the eggs. Top that with some olive oil and grated cheese and you've got a solid breakfast or a nice little snack.

3 (6-ounce) ladles Cooked Sauce (page 141)
  (about 2¼ cups)
6 large eggs, plus 1 for good measure
1 teaspoon chopped fresh Italian parsley
Pinch of salt
Pinch of black pepper
2 tablespoons grated pecorino

Take the sauce and heat it up in a small frying pan. Beat the eggs in a medium bowl and throw in the parsley, salt, and pepper.

When the sauce is hot but not boiling, add the egg mixture and turn the heat down to medium. Mix with a fork until the eggs come together, 4 to 5 minutes.

Take the pan off the heat, throw on the pecorino, and serve.

SCHATZ'S LOX, EGGS, AND ONIONS

SERVES 1 TO 2

Fran's mother and father were divorced, and when his mom started dating again, her boyfriend would sometimes sleep over. And when he'd sleep over, Joy always made a great breakfast— so Fran didn't really mind it. One of the guys she used to date, Steve Schatz, was Jewish, and he was the one who showed Fran how to do up a bagel right—with cream cheese and onion and lox. He would also sometimes make this dish, where the lox gets tossed into some scrambled eggs, which makes for nice, salty bites. Not a bad way to win a kid over.

4 large eggs	2 tablespoons salted butter
Pinch of salt	1 medium onion, chopped
Pinch of black pepper	4 slices lox, cut into bite-size pieces

In a medium bowl, beat the eggs and season with the salt and pepper.

Melt the butter in a frying pan over medium-high heat. When it starts to foam, add the onion and cook until translucent but not browned, about 5 minutes. Add the beaten eggs, turning them continuously with a fork or spatula, until they're fluffy and scrambled but still a little soft, 3 to 4 minutes. Remove from the heat, fold in the lox, and serve.

Steve Schatz and Fran's mom

MOONSTRUCK EGGS

SERVES 1 TO 2

One day back in 1987, we wanted to go to the movies. We were with Sal's older sister, Maria, and his brother, Dom, and they wanted to see RoboCop *or* Lethal Weapon, *or somethin' like that. But Fran, he wanted to see* Moonstruck. *We were like, eleven years old, and the kid wanted to see a love story. But Fran knew it took place in Brooklyn, in our parents' old neighborhood. No one else was really into it and Maria was all mad, but it was starting earlier than the other shows that day, so we went. Fran still remembers it like it was yesterday: Maria cracking up the whole time, turning to him and sayin', "I told you I didn't want to see this movie!" She loved it.*

The scene that stood out to us the most, though, was at the end, when Olympia Dukakis is making breakfast for everybody—Cher, Nick Cage, Danny Aiello, Vincent Gardenia—after they'd been out all night, and she started makin' eggs the way our mothers and grandmother did, by cracking an egg in the middle of some bread. We both got home and were like, "Ma! You make that!" It was a big deal.

This is just like Egg in a Basket, except you use slices of Italian bread. And our mothers also dredge the toast in eggs too, so it's almost more like French toast with a fried egg in it.

2 slices Italian bread, cut 1½ inches thick

2 tablespoons salted butter

2 large eggs

Salt and black pepper

Place an upside-down shot glass or juice glass in the center of each slice of bread, and gently twist the glass to make a hole. Remove the cut-out pieces of bread and set aside.

Melt the butter in a medium frying pan over low heat. Add the bread slices and the cut-out circles and let them brown. Flip them over to brown the other side. Remove the bread circles, leaving the slices in the pan.

Crack an egg into the hole of each bread slice. Be careful not to break the yolk! (If you're worried about getting shell in there, crack each egg into a bowl first, without breaking the yolk, and then tip it into the hole in the bread.) Cook the eggs over low

heat until the yolk is no longer runny, then flip the egg and bread together with a spatula and cook for a few more seconds on the other side. Remove from the heat.

Sprinkle each egg with salt and pepper to taste and serve with the toasted bread circles to sop up all that delicious yolk.

Sal's sister, Maria, and Fran's sister Aimee

PANE E LATTE

SERVES 1 HUNGRY GUY

There's nothing much to pane e latte—*or "bread and hot milk" in our house—but it's outta this world. Our grandfather would make it all the time, sometimes having it for breakfast or sometimes as a late-night snack, eating it at the table alone with the lights off. He'd heat up the milk in a pan, pour it over stale bread, put some espresso (or what he called "black coffee") on top, add a little sugar, and eat it hot. If he was making it for us, how much espresso we got depended on how old we were. If you were older, you got a little more black coffee, but if you were younger, you just got a taste (or else you'd be bouncin' off the walls).*

2 cups whole milk

½ loaf day-old (or older) bread from
    your favorite Italian bakery, cut into
    1-inch cubes

2 tablespoons sugar

1 shot espresso (optional)

In a small saucepot, gently heat the milk over low heat until scalding hot.

Place the bread in a bowl and top it with the hot milk, sugar, and espresso (if using). Dig in.

ITALIAN FRENCH TOAST

SERVES 2 TO 4

This was a very, very popular dish in our houses. Not only because it was so good, but because there was always *leftover bread—whether it was from the restaurants or extra from Sunday supper. And in our family, there were three places that bread would go: bread crumbs, pigeon food, or French toast. That's the key to good French toast: It's gotta be dry bread so it can really soak up the egg mixture. The way Fran's mom does it is to slather the finished toast with butter, sprinkle it with sugar, add some jelly, a little more sugar, and then finish it with cinnamon.*

8 large eggs

2 to 2½ cups whole milk

2 teaspoons vanilla extract or amaretto

1 loaf day-old (or older) bread from your favorite
    Italian bakery, cut into 2-inch-thick slices

8 tablespoons (1 stick) salted butter

1 cup packed brown sugar

4 teaspoons ground cinnamon

Grape or raspberry jelly, for serving

In a large bowl, beat together the eggs, milk, and vanilla. Place the bread slices in the egg mixture so they're completely submerged and leave them until they absorb the liquid. Remove the bread and place it on a dish.

Melt 4 tablespoons of the butter in a large frying pan over medium heat. When it starts to foam, add the bread and brown on each side (you may need to work in batches).

Remove the bread from the pan, spread it with more butter, sprinkle it with brown sugar and cinnamon, and finish it off with jelly.

Sal, Fran, and Sal's brother Dominick

3

-HOLDING OUT FOR A HERO-

SANDWICHES

Y ou could say that sandwiches are in our blood. It all started with our grandpa Dominick Casale, who started sellin' heros outta his car. He was working as a longshoreman, so he figured he could make a little extra money sellin' sandwiches. Our grandmother would cook the sandwiches in the house—potatoes and eggs, eggplant, meatball, nothing too expensive to make— then they'd wrap 'em up in waxed paper and sell them right outta the trunk to the dockworkers. They weren't sellin' 'em for more than 50 cents a pop—it was the thirties, after all—but he knew there was money to be made in sandwiches.

In 1961, he opened Chubby Mary's in downtown Brooklyn with our uncle Tommy. Back then, if you were walkin' down Court Street with a hero in your hand and peppers and onions hanging out of it, you can bet you got it at Chubby Mary's. Our grandfather was still workin' down at the piers, though, so that restaurant was short-lived—but there was no gettin' outta the business for our family. You see, our grandfather opened the shop so his sons—our uncles Tommy, Gregory, and Pudgie—could carry it on. Well, Tommy *hated* working in the business. He joined the *army*, he hated it so much! And Pudgie moved down to Miami and opened a big restaurant there—Casale's Alley. He called it that because you had to drive to the back of the lot to get to the entrance. The best part? They shared parking with the Playboy Club next door. Our moms, who went down there to help their brother open the place, would watch the Bunnies smoke cigarettes during their breaks, when they weren't busy preppin' hundreds of glasses of shrimp cocktails for dinner service.

But our uncle Gregory, he understood the power of the sandwich. And let us tell you somethin': It didn't get much better than Uncle Greg. We remember, clear as day, Uncle Greg sittin' outside one of his jewelry shops, holdin' up one of those big mirrors in front of his face to get a suntan, with a big beautiful chain and a big beautiful watch and that beautiful '66 'Vette parked right there. He had an Olympic-size pool in his house in Todt Hill (the Bel Air of Staten Island) and for his twenty-fifth wedding anniversary, he took twenty-five people to Vegas. To us, he was the epitome of cool.

He'd done well in the jewelry business, so when Chubby Mary's closed, he figured he'd open a few restaurants too. He opened three sandwich shops—all called Greg's Heros— one on Hamilton Avenue, one on Clinton Street, and the third on Van Brunt Street. They did some heros, some hot plates, and a whole lot of rice puddin'. But it wasn't Uncle Greg who made those places magic—it was the ladies. Greg mighta been the one to start the business, but it was his wife, Loulou, her twin sister, Gilda, and all their friends who made Greg's run like it did.

Every morning, our aunt Loulou and Gilda—who lived with Loulou and Greg because she was widowed young—would wake up and drive to downtown Brooklyn to open one of the shops at five a.m. Now, this was Red Hook back in the day—not exactly a nice neighborhood. But it was a real workingman's place. Every morning, all the factory workers

Uncle Tommy, Uncle Gregory, and Grandpa Dominick

and truck drivers and policemen and scrapyard guys—they all came in to work. And they needed somewhere to eat. And they especially needed somewhere to eat where all the ladies were pretty peroxide blondes who wore their hair all teased up with the big earrings and the makeup and the nails and the little aprons and all that. Sal's mom still remembers how every night the girls would call each other to see which outfit they were all gonna wear the next day. But like we said, those ladies *worked*. These guys would come in and they would need to eat *fast*. Loulou and her crew would move three thousand sandwiches in the span of two hours. They had the 85-cent Special, which was their biggest seller—ham, cheese, lettuce, tomato, and mayo. It was big, too, like twelve inches, and it meant they'd go through something like three cases of ham and two cases of cheese a day. They'd have to pre-slice the cold cuts the night before because they'd be so busy pumpin' out the sandwiches during the lunch rush. Sal's mom swears that's how she knocked her shoulder out. Then they'd slice up all the pies, stick a fork in each slice, and wrap 'em up so people could just grab one on the way out. In the afternoon, they'd get another rush of people who had a fifteen-minute break. The guys from the paint factory and the mattress factory would send the same runner with the same exact order every day. It got to the point where the guy on the grill would start gettin' eggs on the flattop whenever he saw one of them comin' over. Then the girls would line up the coffee cups and mark them—light and sweet, black, etc.—so he could get back in time for the workers to enjoy the rest of their break. And every afternoon at three p.m., they'd close up and head home, because after four p.m., you didn't want to be in that neighborhood anymore. And for thirty years, Loulou, Gilda, and those ladies ran Greg's.

So for us, sandwiches have always been a way of life. Plus, heros were always a good way of gettin' rid of leftovers. Eggplant, ham, turkey, chicken—whatever we had. And that was all right, because just about anything got better when it was tucked between two slices of fresh Cangiano's bread. Some of our fondest memories are of packin' up some heros and driving to the beach in our friend Jared's mother's Riviera. The sand would get into the sandwiches, but it was kinda nice how it added a little crunch. And then there was hanging out on our grandfather's boat all day and just attacking the cooler when it was lunchtime. We'd be starvin' from bein' out on the water so long and couldn't wait to tear into the heros he had made outta last night's dinner. There wasn't a late-night snack or school lunch or hangover that couldn't be cured with a sandwich. As Sal once said, "You could feed a whole family with a loafa bread."

....

COLD SICILIAN-STYLE EGGPLANT ON WONDER BREAD

MAKES 5 SANDWICHES

There were very few meals in our houses at which eggplant wasn't in attendance. As a result, there were always leftovers, and with a little grated cheese between a couple of slices of Wonder Bread (God, thank you for bringing it back), it made the perfect school lunch. Our moms would wrap up our sandwiches in the tinfoil they used at the restaurant, and when we took 'em out of our lunch bags at school, kids looked at us like we had ten heads. But it didn't matter—by the time lunch rolled around and the eggplant had seeped into the bread—makin' it all soggy and delicious—nobody coulda done better than one of these sandwiches.

1 recipe Sicilian Fried Eggplant with the Skin On (page 73)
½ loaf Wonder Bread
½ cup grated pecorino

Lay 3 slices of the eggplant on a slice of bread and sprinkle with some of the cheese. Top with another slice of bread. Repeat until you're outta eggplant or bread.

RICOTTA AND JELLY

MAKES 4 SANDWICHES

When we weren't eatin' cold eggplant for lunch, we sometimes got peanut butter and jelly, like the rest of the kids at school. But one day Fran went over to his buddy Guy Caldovino's house, and his mother, Lucille, made Fran a ricotta (or "riganta," as it's pronounced in our houses) and jelly sandwich. Fran went home and told his mother about it like he'd discovered a new country or somethin'—ricotta and jelly on bread! We always had ricotta in the house, so she started making it for him that way. He's never looked back since.

½ loaf Wonder Bread or fresh Italian bread

2 cups whole-milk ricotta

1 jar of your favorite jelly, jam, or fresh preserves—
    we always like Welch's grape

If using Italian bread, split the bread, then cut it into 4 pieces. Spread a healthy scoop of ricotta on one slice of bread like you're makin' a peanut butter and jelly. Spread some jelly over another slice, slap 'em together, and enjoy.

BROCCOLI RABE HERO

MAKES 2 HEROS

Our uncle Frankie—our motha's motha's brotha—was eccentric. He was nuts. He never married and had nine dogs all named Puppy and seven cats. He used to make these S-shaped cookies and they would always have cat hair in 'em. And he would just scream bloody murder at the top of his lungs at these cats and dogs. You could hear him from three blocks away. Anyways, every Sunday he would walk over the Brooklyn Bridge to go to the Cammareri Bros. bakery on Sackett and Henry to buy bread. You know the one—where Nick Cage filmed his big Moonstruck *scene ("Bring me the big knife!"). Frankie would take the ferry back, and our grandfather would go pick him up and bring him over to the house. He had to get picked up because he never figured out how to drive. When he moved to Staten Island from Brooklyn, he finally got his driver's license and bought a '75 Mustang—the year Ford made some really ugly Mustangs. But it was bright red and in mint condition like it was right out of a magazine. Thing is, though, by the time he got it home from the dealership, it was all smashed up. The hood was bashed in, the fender all*

Uncle Frankie

messed up, a coupla dents in the roof. He'd be out there crashing into parked cars and everything. He went and got his car all fixed up, but he wrecked it again. At one point the cops just followed him home to make sure he didn't crash into anything else. The guy couldn't drive.

Crazy as he mighta been, though, that bread he picked up from Cammareri's was the best. And when you have good bread, some broccoli rabe sautéed in garlic and oil until it's nice and soft, and pecorino—it's the most delicious thing you could eat. We serve this in our hero shop, and people are always surprised to see broccoli rabe on a sandwich. But in our family, it was a popular thing, a very Sicilian thing to eat, real peasant food. And once people try it, they love it. Plus, when you start eatin' these and stop havin' chicken cutlets or sausage, you start losin' a little weight.

CONTINUED

¼ cup olive oil

2 tablespoons chopped garlic

1 teaspoon salt

Pinch of red pepper flakes

2 pounds broccoli rabe (like the Andy Boy
bundles), bottom inch of the stems removed
and the rest cut into roughly 2-inch pieces

½ cup chicken stock

12 kalamata olives, pitted

1 loaf good crusty Italian bread

½ cup grated pecorino

In a frying pan, heat the oil over medium heat. Add the garlic, salt, and red pepper flakes.
Cook until the garlic is lightly browned. Add the broccoli rabe and sauté for a minute or
two. Add the chicken stock and olives, cover, and let simmer until tender. Spread the
mixture on the bread and let all the juices get absorbed. Sprinkle with the pecorino and
serve hot.

ANCHOVIES AND TOMATO ON WHITE TOAST

MAKES 2 SANDWICHES

*We remember our grandfather, clear as day, sittin' at his table when we were kids and takin'
one, two, even three tins of anchovies, puttin' 'em on regular ol' white bread, and eatin' 'em just
like that. He was a hard-core anchovy extremist. We would try a bite and remember thinkin' it
was the worst thing we ever tasted. But our grandfather, he knew better. He was always sayin',
"I gotta teach you how to eat. I'll show you how to run your plate, kid." Obviously, he did a good
job. As teens we started tryin' anchovies on pizza and realized that they ain't so bad. And
layered on some good toasted bread with tomatoes, they give you that delicious umami flavor.
Looks like we finally got our plates right.*

1 can Italian-style anchovies

4 slices white bread, toasted

1 ripe medium tomato, sliced

Black pepper

For each sandwich, take 4 or 5 anchovies and lay them on a piece of the toast. Top with
half the sliced tomatoes and drizzle with some of the oil from the anchovy tin, then close
the sandwich with a second piece of toast. Season with pepper to taste.

MEATBALL AND PEPPERS HERO

MAKES 2 HEROS

Years after the original Chubby Mary's closed, our grandfather opened another hero shop called Bella's, named after Sal's mom. It was on Clinton Street, underneath the BQE, right by the projects. It had a cold station, a pizza station, and a hot station with a big steam table. When we were kids, we were allowed to go back there and eat, mixin' up whatever we wanted on our plates. Our grandfather, he'd always put the peppers and onions with the meatballs, which was kinda unusual, because normally you'd put the peppers and onions with sausage. Well, we started doin' it too, just like he did it—puttin' the pepper juice down on the bread first to baste it, which gave it so much flavor. We made sure to have this on our menu at the new Chubby Mary's as a tribute, and it got real popular real fast.

4 to 6 small to medium bell peppers (any color)

¼ cup olive oil

Salt and black pepper

2 hero rolls from your favorite Italian bakery

6 Grandma's Meatballs (page 213)

2 cups Cooked Sauce (page 141)

½ cup grated pecorino

Wash the peppers, cut them in half, and clean out the seeds. Cut them into strips and dry them with a paper towel.

In a large frying pan, heat the olive oil over medium-high heat until it shimmers. Add the pepper slices, cover the pan, and cook for 5 minutes. Remove the lid and stir the peppers with a wooden spoon. Add the salt and black pepper to taste, and continue cooking with the lid off until the peppers are soft, about 10 minutes more.

Slice the hero rolls in half and fill each with 3 meatballs, 1 cup sauce, and a whole lot of the peppers. Sprinkle with the pecorino and enjoy hot.

FORGOTTEN FISH

MAKES 1 SANDWICH

Today, most people have never even heard of a sardine sandwich. But back in the day, it was popular. Used to be that people always had sardines in their pantries. Then in the seventies, once tuna in the can came around, people started buying that instead. We're guessin' it's because sardines were considered peasant food—what our grandparents and their parents grew up eatin' when it was all they could afford. Fran's father, though, he loved makin' sardine sandwiches with lettuce, tomato, onions, mayo, and mustard. Try it and you'll wonder why people ever stopped.

3 tablespoons mayonnaise

½ loaf fresh Italian bread, halved lengthwise

2 tablespoons brown mustard (we like Gulden's)

2 cans brisling sardines

1 small white onion, thinly sliced

1 small ripe tomato, sliced

2 tablespoons olive oil

Salt and black pepper

Spread mayo on one half of the bread and mustard on the other. Arrange the sardines on one half and the onion, tomato slices, and olive oil on the other. Season with salt and pepper to taste, close the sandwich, and serve.

PANELLE SPECIAL

(SICILIAN FRITTER WITH RICOTTA AND SHAVED PARMIGIANO-REGGIANO ON A SOFT ROUND ROLL)

MAKES 6 SANDWICHES

Over on Union Street in Carroll Gardens, Brooklyn, there's a place called Ferdinando's Focacceria. It's been there forever—since 1888; our grandmothers used to go there as little girls. It's an institution and everyone from our part of Staten Island knows about it—especially about their panelle, *or fried chickpea dough. It's kinda like a potato pancake, but all there is to it is garbanzo bean flour. Used to be that only peasants in Italy would eat* panelle, *and if you were lucky enough to have a cow, you would throw some ricotta on it. At Ferdinando's, though, we all ate like kings because they'd finish it off with a nice scoop of ricotta and a handful of Parmigiano, then pile it on a big seeded roll and toast the whole thing. Beautiful.*

2½ cups olive oil, plus more for the pan

2 cups vegetable oil

1 teaspoon salt

8 ounces (or 1¾ cups) garbanzo bean flour

6 soft round Italian rolls

1 (32-ounce) container whole-milk ricotta

1 (4-ounce) piece Parmigiano-Reggiano, thinly shaved

Coat a glass loaf pan (such as Pyrex) or an empty quart-size ricotta container with 1 teaspoon olive oil and 1 teaspoon water. Set aside.

In a medium saucepot, combine 1½ cups of the olive oil, 1 cup of the vegetable oil, 4 cups cold water, and the salt and set the pot over low heat. Sift the flour into the pot while whisking continuously to make sure no lumps form while the mixture cooks. It will start to look like cooked farina.

When the mixture reaches a boil and starts pulling away from the sides of the pot, pull it off the stove but continue whisking as you pour the dough into the greased loaf pan.

Cover the loaf pan with plastic wrap pressed directly on top of the dough. This will prevent a hard crust from forming. Let the dough cool at room temperature for about an hour, hour and a half until the mixture sets.

Preheat the oven to 350°F. Line a plate with paper towels.

Unmold the dough onto a clean baking sheet or large cutting board. It will look like an uncooked loaf of bread. Slice the dough into 1-inch-thick slices.

In a large frying pan, combine 1 cup vegetable oil and 1 cup olive oil and heat on high. Test the heat by throwing in a little bit of dough—if it sizzles, the oil is ready. Lay a few slices of dough in the hot oil and fry until golden brown. Be sure not to crowd the pan; otherwise, the dough will steam instead of getting crispy. Cook the panelle in batches if you have to.

Flip the panelle over and brown on the other side. Transfer to the paper towel–lined plate and let cool slightly.

To assemble the sandwiches, put 2 to 3 panelle slices on a roll and top with ricotta and some Parmigiano-Reggiano. Put the sandwiches on a baking sheet and bake until the rolls are slightly toasted but the ricotta's still a little cold, about 2 to 3 minutes.

GARBANZO BEAN FLOUR

Garbanzo bean flour is made by grinding dried garbanzo beans, also commonly known as chickpeas or ceci beans (pronounced "chichi"), as they were called in our houses. This flour can be found in the baking aisle in most supermarkets and is sometimes labeled "gram" flour.

MANHATTAN SPECIAL

Another thing that makes Ferdinando's so special is that it's one of the only places in the country that has Manhattan Special on tap. Made in Williamsburg, it's an espresso soda that was basically the Red Bull of the sixties and seventies. You drink one and you're beamin'. At Ferdinando's, to this day, you order a Manhattan Special and the waitress goes over to a block of ice and chips some off the old-fashioned way with an ice pick.

FRIED SALAMI SANDWICH

MAKES 1 SANDWICH

We used to go to Christina's Café—a Staten Island restaurant that closed about eight years ago—just to get this. The owner would usually be sittin' outside readin' the paper with a big cigar and a little cup of espresso. We think he owned the place just because he liked to hang out there. But there were certain things that he would get up to make, and this was one of 'em. Most of the time, he'd just be out front while the guys in the kitchen cooked. But if you ordered a fried salami sandwich, he'd get up—lookin' all annoyed—and cook one for you. First, he'd take a fryin' pan and put some salami in there just to crisp it up a little, like bacon. Then he'd put it on a piece of toasted Italian bread with some caramelized onions, Russian dressing, and Muenster cheese—kinda like a Reuben but with salami instead of corned beef. It was outta this world.

¼ pound thinly sliced Genoa salami

1 tablespoon olive oil

1 small red onion, sliced

½ loaf fresh Italian bread, halved lengthwise

1 ripe large tomato, sliced

3 slices Muenster cheese

5 fresh basil leaves, torn

¼ cup Thousand Island dressing

Preheat the oven to 400°F.

In a medium skillet, cook the salami slices over medium heat until they sizzle. Remove them from the pan and set aside.

Add the oil and onion to the skillet and sauté until the onion is soft, 4 to 5 minutes.

To assemble the sandwich, layer some salami on half the bread and top with the tomato slices, sautéed onions, cheese, and basil. Top with the other half of the bread. Put the sandwich on a baking sheet and bake for 3 to 5 minutes, until the bread is slightly brown and toasted and the cheese has melted. Top with Thousand Island dressing and eat hot.

THIS WAY, THAT WAY, AND THE OTHER THING

Back in 2009, we opened up This Little Piggy Had Roast Beef in Manhattan. We wanted to keep the menu small—or let's call it specialized—*and focus on roast beef and pastrami. When we first opened, we had three sandwiches: This Way, That Way, and The Other Thing. There wasn't anything particularly Italian about them—except maybe the bread—but these sandwiches were our way of sayin' thanks to some of our favorite hero shops.*

THIS WAY: ROAST BEEF WITH AU JUS AND CHEEZ WHIZ
MAKES 1 SANDWICH

Whenever we went to Coney Island for the rides—if we were lucky—Fran's father or our uncle Greg would take us to Sheepshead Bay to go to Roll-N-Roaster and get roast beef au jus with Cheez Whiz on a good roll. It was so simple, but the place was always jam-packed. When we moved to the city, we couldn't believe that no one had anything like it.

Olive oil

½ small red onion, sliced

1 garlic clove, chopped

1 (8-ounce) can beef broth

½ tablespoon all-purpose flour

Salt and black pepper

1 hard roll, like a kaiser roll, split

⅛ pound thinly sliced roast beef

1 (8-ounce) jar Cheez Whiz

First, make the jus—which is just a fancy way of saying "sauce that tastes awesome with roast beef." Coat the bottom of a large skillet with olive oil and get it hot over medium-high heat. Add the onion slices and let them brown, 5 to 7 minutes. Add the garlic and sauté until lightly brown, about 2 minutes.

Add the beef broth and bring it to a low boil. Simmer for 15 minutes. Strain the broth through a fine-mesh strainer into a bowl; discard the solids in the strainer. Return the jus to the skillet and set it over medium heat. Whisk in the flour and simmer, whisking frequently to make sure there aren't any lumps, for 5 minutes. Season with salt and pepper to taste.

Dunk both cut sides of the roll into the jus, then place them on a plate. Pile the bottom half of the roll high with roast beef, smother with Cheez Whiz, and close with the top of the roll. Serve with the remaining jus for dipping.

THAT WAY: ROAST BEEF WITH BROWN GRAVY AND FRESH MOZZARELLA
MAKES 1 SANDWICH

Over at John's Deli, which first opened in Brooklyn and then in Staten Island, they served up their roast beef fresh—cooked that day—and made sandwiches Brooklyn-style: toasted Italian bread, fresh mozzarella, roast beef, and black gravy. At our shop, we cooked the roast beef nice and simple with onions, salt, and pepper, then used the drippings to make the gravy. But in a pinch you can use Gravy Master to get that deep beefy flavor.

Olive oil

1 small white onion, sliced

1 garlic clove, chopped

1 (8-ounce) can beef broth

½ tablespoon all-purpose flour

1 teaspoon Gravy Master

Salt and black pepper

½ loaf fresh Italian bread, halved lengthwise

¼ pound thinly sliced roast beef (8 slices)

½ small ball fresh mozzarella, sliced

First, make the gravy. Coat the bottom of a large skillet with olive oil and get it hot over medium-high heat. Add the onion and garlic and sauté until lightly brown. Remove half of the onion-garlic mixture and set aside.

Add the beef broth to the pan, bring to a low boil, then reduce the heat to maintain a simmer and cook for 10 minutes.

Strain the broth mixture through a strainer into a bowl, then return it to the pan; discard any solids in the strainer. Whisk in the flour and Gravy Master and simmer for 5 minutes, whisking to making sure there aren't any lumps. Season with salt and pepper to taste.

Pour the gravy over both halves of the bread. Layer the roast beef on one half and top with the mozzarella. Finish with another coating of gravy and the sautéed onion and garlic and top with the other half of the bread.

THE OTHER THING: PASTRAMI ON RYE WITH COLESLAW AND MUSTARD
MAKES 1 SANDWICH

Fran's mother, she loves pastrami. We remember when we were really young, her boss took her to Katz's Deli on the Lower East Side and taught her how to eat pastrami with coleslaw and mustard on rye. From then on, that's how she'd eat it, and that's how she served it to us.

We knew we had to add this sandwich to our menu, but first we had to figure out how to even come close to Katz's pastrami. Theirs is, without a doubt, the best you ever ate. We didn't grow up in the deli business, so we had to sample every single pastrami on the market until we could figure out which one they were usin'. We tried every meat distributor, everybody's pastrami, until bingo—we found it. Then all we had to do was steam it to death. The store opened at eleven a.m., so from about eight a.m. until then, the pastrami was workin', until it reached the point where you just had to look at it and it broke apart.

¼ pound thinly sliced pastrami

Brown mustard, preferably Gulden's

2 slices rye bread

¼ cup store-bought coleslaw

Lay the pastrami in a small frying pan and warm on both sides over medium heat for 2 to 3 minutes.

Spread the mustard liberally over the bread and top with the pastrami and coleslaw.

Fran's dad, Frankie, Uncle Gregory, and Aunt Loulou

4.

IT'S THE LITTLE THINGS IN LIFE

APPETIZERS, SIDE DISHES, AND IN-BETWEENS

Whenever there was a family gathering, no matter whose house it was at, there was always somethin' to eat before there was somethin' to eat. At our uncle Greg's house, our aunt Loulou would be fryin' up cauliflower fritters and we'd literally be eating 'em as they came outta the pan. As soon as they hit the paper towel to cool, we'd snatch 'em up. Probably about half of 'em actually made it to the table. But it wasn't like the family went hungry. There'd be a smorgasbord of all different starters and sides—stuffed mushrooms, baked clams, escarole fritters—all ready to go before the macaroni came out.

CAULIFLOWER FRITTERS

SERVES 6

Our aunt Loulou is right up there with our moms and grandmother as one of the best cooks in the family. She and her twin sister, Gilda, ran Greg's Heros down on Van Brunt Street in Brooklyn—just two blond Staten Island girls feedin' truck drivers and working guys every day. They'd open at five a.m. and close at three p.m. and served really hearty food—ham and eggs, chicken marsala, chicken rollatini. And they were famous for making these fritters. Loulou would always bring them to our grandfather's house on Sundays and to every holiday party. That was her thing. She smoked six to eight packs of cigarettes a day, lighting one Virginia Slim and taking two, three drags before lighting another one. We never saw anything like it. She'd be smokin' cigarettes while she was fryin' up the cauliflower, gettin' ashes in the pan. And she'd be droppin' little bits of food for her Lhasa apso, Gizmo. That Gizmo, he ate really good.

But anytime she made these fritters, we'd get so excited. They went down so easy, you know? You could eat five, six of them at a time because they're light. And it's cauliflower, so it's healthy, right? We've seen fried cauliflower on other menus, but not the way we do it. It's usually just a piece of cauliflower that's deep-fried with nothing else really going on. These, though—these are what flew out the door when we opened our first shop. So we figured it was a good idea to make 'em for a James Beard event we did a few years ago. There we were, cookin' alongside chefs like Mario Batali and Michael White for people who paid $8,000 for tickets just to eat our food— and we were makin' fried cauliflower. These fritters were hands down the most popular dish of the night. People begged us for that recipe, and we wouldn't give it up. But we're givin' it to you now. You're gonna love 'em.

6 teaspoons salt

1 head cauliflower, stem and leaves trimmed

4 large eggs

1 teaspoon black pepper

6 tablespoons minced garlic

½ cup chopped fresh flat-leaf parsley

2 cups grated pecorino

2 cups all-purpose flour

2 cups olive oil, for frying

CONTINUED

Bring a medium saucepot of water to a boil. Add 2 teaspoons of the salt and the whole head of cauliflower (quartered if you're using a small pot) and cook until tender and easily pierced with a fork, 15 to 20 minutes. Remove from the water and let cool.

Transfer the cauliflower to a medium bowl and mash with a fork until chunky. Add in the eggs, pepper, garlic, parsley, and cheese. Stir well, then add the flour and remaining 4 teaspoons salt. Mix until well combined.

In a frying pan, heat the olive oil over high heat until it registers about 325°F on a deep-frying thermometer. You can also test the oil without using a thermometer by dropping in a little bit of batter. If it sinks to the bottom or sticks to the side without bubbling, then it isn't ready yet. It's gotta float right to the top and start bubblin' right away.

Scoop ½-cup portions of the batter into the hot oil. Press down on the fritters as they cook with a spatula or spoon so they flatten into disks. Cook evenly on both sides until golden brown. Remove and lay gently on paper towels to absorb the excess oil. Serve hot.

....

VARIATIONS:

ESCAROLE FRITTERS
SERVES 6

Whenever Aunt Loulou made cauliflower fritters, she made these too.

6 teaspoons salt

2 heads escarole, tough stems trimmed
    and leaves cut into 2-inch pieces

4 large eggs

1 teaspoon black pepper

6 tablespoons minced garlic

½ cup chopped fresh Italian parsley

2 cups grated pecorino

2 cups all-purpose flour

2 cups olive oil, for frying

Bring a medium saucepot of water to a boil. Add 2 teaspoons of the salt and the escarole and cook until tender or easily pierced with a fork. Remove the escarole from the water and let it cool.

In a medium bowl, combine the escarole, eggs, pepper, garlic, parsley, and cheese. Stir well, then add the flour and remaining 4 teaspoons salt. Stir until the batter is smooth.

In a frying pan, heat the olive oil over high heat until it registers about 325°F on a deep-frying thermometer. You can also test the oil without using a thermometer by dropping in a little bit of batter. If it sinks to the bottom or sticks to the side without bubbling, then it ain't ready yet. It's gotta float right to the top and start bubbling right away.

Scoop ½-cup portions of the batter into the hot oil and cook them evenly on both sides until they're golden brown, about 2 minutes a side. Remove the fritters from the pan and lay them gently on paper towels to absorb the excess oil. Serve 'em hot.

....

ARTICHOKE FRITTERS
SERVES 6

These weren't on the table as much as cauliflower or escarole fritters, but when we opened Artichoke Pizza, of course we had to have 'em on the menu.

1 (14-ounce) can artichoke hearts (about 30 hearts)

4 large eggs

1 teaspoon black pepper

6 tablespoons minced garlic

½ cup chopped fresh Italian parsley

2 cups grated pecorino

2 cups all-purpose flour

2 tablespoons salt

2 cups olive oil, for frying

In a medium bowl, combine the artichoke hearts, eggs, pepper, garlic, parsley, and cheese. Stir well, then add the flour and salt. Mix the batter until it's smooth.

In frying pan, heat the olive oil over high heat until it registers about 325°F on a deep-frying thermometer. You can also test the oil without using a thermometer by dropping in a little bit of batter. If it sinks to the bottom or sticks to the side without bubbling, then it ain't ready yet. It's gotta float right to the top and start bubbling right away.

Scoop ½-cup portions of the batter into the hot oil and cook them evenly on both sides until they're golden brown, about 2 minutes a side. Remove them from the pan and lay them gently on paper towels to absorb the excess oil. Serve 'em hot.

SOPRESSATA AND PROVOLONE

In our houses, if you had company—even if it was someone just stoppin' over for a quick meetin'—you always had to feed 'em. We always had cheese and cured meat in the fridge, so that was somethin' you could put together in no time. You'd have some provolone, some olives, and some sopressata, which is a spicy, dry salami. You'd get it all on a cuttin' board, maybe with a loaf of bread, and put it on the table for a fast snack or an appetizer before meals, especially during the holidays. It's a great way to feed people quick if dinner's still on the stove. Or keep it in the glove compartment for when you get stuck in traffic on the Verrazano Bridge.

½ pound sliced sopressata

¼ pound sliced provolone

1 jar roasted red peppers

1 large crispy Italian hero roll, halved lengthwise

Spicy brown mustard such as Gulden's

Olive oil

Stack the meat, cheese, and peppers on the hero roll, dress it for success, and get down!

BROCCOLI RABE AND SAUSAGE

SERVES 8 TO 10

Broccoli rabe is grown in Sicily, which is why our family is crazy for the stuff. It's more like a leafy green than like actual broccoli, and it's a little bitter. But after you cook it up with some oil and garlic and serve it with grilled sausage, you don't feel like someone's makin' you eat your vegetables. We eventually grew up to love it after bein' forced to eat it all the time when we were little.

This dish was usually on the table on the weekends when the family was gettin' together. And in the summertime, we'd have it on the barbecue in our grandfather's backyard. We'd get pork sausage from Ariemma's Italian Deli, where they stuffed it with parsley and grated cheese and looped it into a giant pinwheel that was like ten inches across and held together by two skewers like a cross. The secret was cookin' it over a low flame so the outside wouldn't burn before the inside was done.

2 pounds sweet Italian sausage links

3 tablespoons chopped garlic

¼ cup olive oil

2 bunches broccoli rabe, bottom inch
   of the stems trimmed and the rest cut
   into roughly 2-inch pieces

2 cups chicken broth

½ teaspoon red pepper flakes

½ cup grated pecorino

1 lemon, cut into wedges

Preheat the oven to 350°F.

Put the sausage links on a baking sheet and bake for 15 minutes, or until golden brown.

Meanwhile, in a large saucepan, sauté the chopped garlic in the olive oil over medium heat until the garlic begins to brown. Add the broccoli rabe, chicken broth, and red pepper flakes to the pan and cook until the broccoli rabe is tender, about 10 minutes. Transfer the broccoli rabe to a serving bowl.

Slice the cooked sausages into ½-inch rounds, toss them with the broccoli rabe, and serve hot with the grated cheese and a wedge of lemon.

FAST MUSHROOMS

SERVES 2 TO 3

This is a recipe that sorta came to us by accident. When we were working at our mothers' restaurant in Staten Island, something we did was make all the pizza toppings in-house. We weren't using mushrooms that came out of a can, you know? The onions, the mushrooms, the broccoli—it was all sautéed with garlic and olive oil. But sometimes we'd be runnin' low on mushrooms and have to try a little shortcut. We figured out that if you cut 'em nice and thick and put 'em in a hot deep fryer for twenty seconds, they don't shrink to nothin' like they do when they're sautéed in a pan. It's like all the flavor and juiciness were getting locked in because it was so hot and quick.

Now, if you take those hot, steamin' mushrooms, drizzle 'em with a little bit of olive oil, raw garlic, salt, red pepper flakes, a little bit of parsley, and some pecorino? People'll go nuts for 'em.

2 cups olive oil

1 (8-ounce) package button mushrooms, cut into thirds

4 tablespoons chopped garlic

3 tablespoons chopped fresh flat-leaf parsley

2 pinches of salt

1 teaspoon red pepper flakes

½ cup grated pecorino

In a frying pan, heat the olive oil over high heat until it registers 400°F on a deep-frying thermometer. Test to see if the oil's hot enough by dropping a tiny bit of water into the pan. It should sizzle loudly. Add the mushrooms in batches—so you don't crowd the pan and steam 'em—and let 'em flash-fry for 45 seconds, or until tender. Scoop 'em out of the oil with a spider or a slotted spoon and transfer to a bowl. Throw in the garlic, parsley, salt, and red pepper flakes and mix well. Top with the pecorino and serve hot.

SICILIAN FRIED EGGPLANT WITH THE SKIN ON

SERVES 3

While there was no shortage of eggplant on our table, this was the version that was always there. Battered, fried, and layered with pecorino, it was really somethin'. You'd let it cool to room temperature, and the consistency would become almost like caponata or eggplant parm.

4 large eggs

2 cups all-purpose flour

1 teaspoon salt

1 cup olive oil

1 medium eggplant, ends trimmed,
    cut into ¼-inch-thick rounds

1 cup Cooked Sauce (page 141)

¼ cup grated pecorino

In a large bowl, beat together the eggs, flour, salt, and 1 cup water until smooth.

Heat the olive oil in a large saucepan over medium heat until it sizzles. Dip each eggplant slice into the batter and fry in the hot oil until golden brown, about 3 minutes a side. Transfer the eggplant to a paper towel to cool.

To serve, top each piece of eggplant with a couple of big spoonfuls of sauce and sprinkle with some pecorino.

EGGPLANT CHIPS

SERVES 3

Sometimes Fran's mom would slice up some eggplant paper-thin and fry it until it was well done and crispy, almost burnt. She would serve it just like that, with no sauce, just a sprinkling of pecorino. The best part was the skin, which would get all caramelized. They were like the most delicious, addictive potato chips you could ever eat. If you want to get the slices extra thin, use a mandoline to cut 'em.

2 cups olive oil, for frying

1 large eggplant, ends trimmed,
    cut into 1/8-inch-thick rounds

1/4 cup grated pecorino

Heat the olive oil in a frying pan over high heat to about a zillion degrees (or, really, until it registers 400°F on a deep-frying thermometer). Add the eggplant slices and fry until golden brown on both sides, 1 to 2 minutes per side. Don't put too many in the pan at one time or they'll steam instead of fry. Scoop 'em out of the oil with a spider strainer or a slotted spoon and transfer 'em to paper towels to drain. Sprinkle with cheese and serve hot.

FRIED RICE BALLS

MAKES 12 BALLS

You want to know who used to make a mean rice ball? Uncle Tony, our grandmother's brother. He was famous for 'em. He worked at the pastry shop with his father—our great-grandfather—and he'd bake and he'd cook. It's a good thing, too, because his wife, our aunt Dee, was probably 9,000 pounds. Our grandfather used to call her Rikers Island. "You gotta go pick up Rikers Island," he'd say. "Watch out, she's gonna break the car." It was funny because Uncle Tony, he couldn't have been more than five-foot-two and 130 pounds soaking wet. We heard he actually had to put cinder blocks under the bed because she was always breakin' the bed frame.

Anyways, we make a pretty mean rice ball too. We make 'em big like softballs and we call them "Sicilian-style" because they got meat and peas inside. People in Sicily might think we're nuts for callin' 'em that, but at Ferdinando's Focacceria, if you order Sicilian-style, you get meat and peas in the middle. The ingredients are so simple—if you've got leftover meatballs, use 'em. If you've got a pot of sauce, throw a scoop of sauce in there. Or just brown up some chopped meat and throw a can of Contadina in there. We really like usin' provolone inside because it melts really nice with the rice and doesn't get gummy like mozzarella. The other secret is usin' warm rice if you're gonna make 'em and eat 'em the same day. That way, you won't have to burn the daylights outta the outside to get 'em heated through.

Sure, these can be kind of a pain to make, but if there's ever a time to do it, make 'em special as an appetizer for the holidays.

1 (2½-pound) bag white rice, preferably Carolina

1½ cups chicken broth

2 cups shredded provolone

2 cups grated pecorino

2½ cups Cooked Sauce (page 141)

Black pepper

2 tablespoons olive oil

9 ounces ground beef

1 cup green peas

½ white onion, finely chopped

2 teaspoons chopped garlic

Salt

Pinch of chopped fresh flat-leaf parsley

2 quarts soybean oil, for frying

2 cups all-purpose flour

12 large eggs

2 cups whole milk

2 cups Dry Bread Crumbs (recipe on page 79)

CONTINUED

In a large saucepot, combine 3½ quarts water with the rice and chicken broth. Bring to a boil over high heat, reduce the heat to low, cover, and simmer until the rice is soft and the liquid has been absorbed, 15 to 20 minutes.

Stir in the provolone, pecorino, 1½ cups of the Cooked Sauce, and 1 tablespoon pepper. The rice should turn a pretty orange color and the consistency should be like glue—you should be able to use it to repair brickwork. Remove the pot from the heat.

In a frying pan, heat the olive oil over high heat. Add the meat, peas, onion, garlic, 3 pinches of salt, 2 pinches of pepper, and the parsley. Cook until the mixture is browned, then carefully drain the grease from the pan.

Once the rice has cooled just enough to not burn you, use your hands to form it into softball-size balls (about 12 ounces each). For each rice ball, scoop about 1 tablespoon of the meat mixture and 1 tablespoon of the Cooked Sauce into the middle, then roll the rice around the filling in your hands until it's entirely round.

In a large saucepot, heat the soybean oil over medium heat until it's sizzling.

While the oil is heating, set up a breading station for the rice balls: Put the flour into a medium bowl. Next, in another large bowl, beat together the eggs and milk. Put the bread crumbs in a third bowl.

To bread each rice ball, first roll it in the flour until well coated. Next, soak it in the egg mixture, then transfer it immediately to the bowl with the bread crumbs and roll it around to coat generously. Repeat until all the rice balls are breaded.

Fry each rice ball in the hot oil for 3 minutes on each side, or until golden brown. Transfer them to paper towels to drain and cool slightly. Serve warm.

DRY BREAD CRUMBS

MAKES 4 CUPS

When our grandfather wasn't cookin' or bottlin' sauce or picklin' eggplant, he was makin' bread crumbs. He was big on making his own because he thought it was better for his meatballs. He was good friends with the guys down at Melone & Sons Bakery in Staten Island—an institution to this day, even though our grandfather would joke that their bread was only good half the time because Bobby Melone was only half Italian. But they really did make delicious bread. He'd go down there on Sunday and they'd give him all the bread they didn't sell. Then he'd cut it into cubes, dry it out in the sun, season it with grated cheese, salt, pepper, and parsley; ziplock it up; and give a bag to everybody to take home after they came over to eat. When Sal was in college in Florida and our grandpa had moved out there, he always sent Sal home from his visits with a bag so Sal could make some decent meals in the dorms. In fact, every weekend Sal would cook Sunday dinner for everybody because he was the only Italian kid. That bag of bread crumbs would last him all semester—it was like gold.

4 cups unseasoned bread crumbs, made using
   our grandfather's method or store-bought

1 cup grated pecorino

3 tablespoons salt

4 tablespoons dried parsley

2 tablespoons black pepper

2 tablespoons granulated garlic

In a large bowl, toss all the ingredients together and combine well. These'll keep in an airtight bag for years.

STUFFED MUSHROOMS

WITH RICOTTA AND SECRET BREAD CRUMBS

SERVES 6

Most people, when they make stuffed mushrooms, they take the stem out, chop it up, and mix it with onions and bread crumbs to make a stuffing. But us? We think we can do better. First, we take the stem out and put a scoop of ricotta right in there with some pecorino and heap our Secret Bread Crumbs (page 82) over the top. Then we put a little oil and garlic and a shot of white wine in the pan with the mushrooms, so the mushrooms get nice and flavorful when they cook. And we cook 'em in a nice, hot oven so the mushrooms don't get all dried out. Instead, in just a few minutes they get a little crispy, but still have some body to them. It's no wonder these are so famous at Artichoke.

24 cremini mushrooms

16 ounces ricotta cheese, or cream cheese, if you want to change it up a bit

½ cup grated pecorino

1 batch Secret Bread Crumbs (recipe on page 82)

1 cup chicken stock

½ cup olive oil

1 cup white wine, preferably Chardonnay

½ bunch fresh flat-leaf parsley, leaves and stems chopped

3 tablespoons chopped garlic

1 tablespoon red pepper flakes

Preheat the oven to broil.

Scoop out the stems from the mushroom caps and fill each mushroom with a heaping teaspoon of ricotta and a good pinch of pecorino. Then, top each mushroom with a dollop of Secret Bread Crumbs.

Arrange the mushrooms, with the filling facing up, in a shallow baking pan. Pour in the chicken stock, olive oil, and wine and sprinkle with the parsley, garlic, and red pepper flakes. Broil the mushrooms for 10 to 15 minutes, or until they're golden brown.

CONTINUED

SECRET BREAD CRUMBS

MAKES ABOUT 6 CUPS

In the restaurant, we always had two types of bread crumbs. The first kind was dry bread crumbs—ground up old bread, grated cheese, dried parsley, salt, pepper, and granulated garlic. You'd use them to bread cutlets or shrimp or eggplant. But if you wanted to stuff things like fish oreganata, chicken oreganata, peppers, or mushrooms, then you'd use these, which were Grandma Maria Basille's creation. First, you add your fresh garlic, your grated cheese, your olive oil, your salt, your pepper. Then, you add the secret ingredient: a couple of scoops of sauce. Ta-da! It gives you a little bit of moisture without making the crumbs greasy, which makes a world of difference. Everybody's always askin' us how we get our bread crumbs that pretty orange color, and we're always sayin', "Sorry, we just can't tell you." But now we're tellin' you.

4 cups unseasoned bread crumbs, made using our grandfather's method (page 79) or store-bought

2 cups grated pecorino

2 cups Cooked Sauce (page 141)

1 cup olive oil

¼ cup salt

1 bunch fresh flat-leaf parsley, leaves and stems chopped

¼ cup chopped pignoli nuts

3 tablespoons chopped garlic

2 tablespoons black pepper

In a large bowl, toss all the ingredients together and combine well. These'll keep, covered, in the fridge for about a week.

Sal's Grandma Maria and Grandma Connie

STUFFED PEPPERS

SERVES 6

Fran had this next-door neighbor, Dominick Narciso, who was like another father to him. A real Italian guy. Like all the other people in the neighborhood, his backyard was almost completely cemented over—because it was easier to clean that way. But every summer, he grew tomatoes, peppers, and basil in these compound buckets. We're not talking about a few of them. No kidding, you would look at this guy's yard and it looked like Frank's Nursery. There were probably five thousand buckets lined up in his yard. He'd even put up shelving so he could fit more buckets out there.

Now, on the other side of Dom's house was our friend Claudia's house. And just like at Fran's, they had an aboveground pool. So we'd reach through the chain-link fence, grab some of Dominick's tomatoes, and try to throw 'em into Claudia's pool. Then they'd pull a few from their side and try to throw 'em into Fran's yard. We probably had three or four of those tomato fights, but one time we really went nuts, stealin' all kinds of tomatoes, and Dom didn't talk to us for like two years. We didn't realize how much work went into growin' those tomatoes!

But for the most part, Dom was happy to share what he grew. He'd bring big bowls of his peppers across the street to our grandparents and over to Fran's house. Talk about locally sourced—we didn't even know we were being cool! We'd eat 'em stuffed with the Secret Bread Crumbs (page 82) and some grated cheese and parsley, then fried on both sides in a pan with just enough oil to coat the bottom. It was like Donnie Brasco said: "Minga, those peppers, forgettaboutit!"

12 green cubanelle peppers, stem ends and seeds removed
4 cups Secret Bread Crumbs (page 82)
2 cups olive oil

Stuff each pepper to the top with Secret Bread Crumbs.

In a large saucepan, heat the olive oil over medium heat until it sizzles. Fry the peppers in the hot oil for 3 minutes on each side. Transfer the peppers to a paper towel to drain and cool slightly. Serve warm.

POTATO CROQUETTES

SERVES 10 TO 11

Our grandmother would make these. They were so good that she was always havin' to smack our hands away, yellin' at us to get out of the fryin' pan. But the potato croquettes that we loved the best were at Ferdinando's Focacceria. They were a staple there, and we got them every time we went—which was a big deal, because we didn't get to go out to eat all the time. They're so greasy, but so good. They don't bread them too thick, so the breading stays crisp against the creamy potatoes. We swore that once we could drive ourselves, we'd go there all the time, so when we got our licenses, that was it.

Here's our version—lucky for you at home we don't peel the potatoes for this recipe.

1 (5-pound) bag small red potatoes

1 cup (2 sticks) salted butter

2 cups grated pecorino

2 cups shredded mozzarella, preferably Polly-O

½ bunch fresh flat-leaf parsley, leaves and stems chopped

2 tablespoons salt

1 tablespoon black pepper

1 quart soybean oil

2 cups all-purpose flour

12 large eggs

2 cups whole milk

2 cups Dry Bread Crumbs (page 79)

Put the potatoes in a large saucepot and add just enough cold water to cover them. Bring the water to a boil, reduce the heat to maintain a simmer, and cook until the potatoes are fork-tender, 10 to 20 minutes (check every 5 minutes after 10 minutes). Drain the potatoes and put them back into the pot.

Add the butter, both cheeses, parsley, salt, and pepper and mix together while smashing the potatoes until the mixture is smooth.

Next, get ready to fry. In a large frying pan, heat the soybean oil over medium heat until it's sizzling hot. Put the flour in one bowl, the eggs and milk (beaten together) in another, and the bread crumbs in a third.

Use an ice cream scooper to portion out the croquettes (about 2½ ounces per croquette). Use your hands to roll the croquettes until they're shaped like a D battery. If you have some of the potato mixture left over, you can power your flashlight with it.

Coat all the croquettes well with flour, soak them in the egg mixture, then transfer them immediately to the bowl with the bread crumbs and coat them generously.

Fry each croquette for 3 minutes on each side or until golden brown. Transfer to paper towels to cool and serve warm.

SICILIAN-STYLE SNAILS IN THE SHELL (BABBALUCI)

SERVES 4

Fran's friend Anthony Garafalo—his mother used to make this. They were Sicilian, straight off the boat. We don't think there was a square inch of that house that wasn't covered with marble or granite. It was like walkin' into a mausoleum. Everything, floor to ceiling—you didn't know where the marble ended and the granite started. And there was plastic on the sofa, the whole deal. You coulda taken a fire hose to that place and nothin' woulda been damaged. It was real Bensonhurst, which is where they lived. Fran and Anthony, they were always fishin' on Anthony's boat, and they always came back to Anthony's to eat—especially for these snails. Anthony's mom would throw the whole thing over some leftover bread, so you'd eat the snails outta the shell first, then eat the sauce with the bread. It was just like at our houses—always findin' ways to use somethin' that was old and not waste it.

You can find nice large snails at some fish markets, but if you're having trouble, you can use the small escargot sold in cans in most supermarkets.

½ cup olive oil

3 garlic cloves, minced

5 cups canned peeled tomatoes, preferably Nina

¼ cup sherry cooking wine

1½ tablespoons chopped fresh flat-leaf parsley

¾ tablespoon chopped fresh basil

Pinch of salt

2 pinches of black pepper

6 tablespoons tomato paste

1 tablespoon salted butter

¼ cup clam juice

6 dozen snails

1 loaf crusty Italian bread

In a medium saucepan, heat the olive oil over medium heat until it shimmers. Add the garlic and cook until it just browns. Add the tomatoes, sherry, parsley, basil, salt, and pepper and cook for 25 minutes.

Stir in the tomato paste and the butter until the butter has melted, then slowly add the clam juice, while stirring, to thin out the sauce. Once the sauce has reached a consistency that's a little thicker, like tomato soup, add the snails and cook for 5 to 7 minutes. Serve hot with crusty Italian bread to soak up the sauce.

SAUCE AND BUTTER HERO

A.K.A. FAT KID'S SPECIAL

MAKES 1 HERO

A lotta times in the morning, if there weren't bagels around, you had Italian bread with your butter and jelly and coffee. And on the weekends, there was a good chance that there was already gravy cookin' on the stove. So we invented this dish as something to eat when the sauce wasn't quite done but you were too hungry to wait for supper. We'd butter a piece of bread and dunk the whole thing in the sauce. The warm gravy would make the butter melt and you'd have this big, greasy bite with sauce runnin' down your arms. It was so good that we put it on our menu at Chubby Mary's.

6 tablespoons Breakstone's salted whipped
    butter (the good stuff)
½ loaf fresh Italian bread, halved lengthwise
½ cup Cooked Sauce (page 141), hot
2 tablespoons grated pecorino

Spread the butter on the bread and toast the bread until the butter melts. Top with hot tomato sauce and cheese, and enjoy.

EGGPLANT WITH AMERICAN

SERVES 10 TO 12

Before Fran's mom, Joy, got into the restaurant business, she worked for lawyers as a secretary. She even worked for Philip Minardo, who's now a New York Supreme Court justice. One of our earliest memories was her catering a party for these guys, since they knew she was a good cook. We remember her gettin' the big catering pans and makin' this dish, which she'd usually make as an hors d'oeuvre if we had a lotta people comin' over. She'd slice the eggplant, batter it, fry it, then layer it with a piece of American cheese and top it with another piece of eggplant—like an eggplant Oreo.

4 large eggs

1½ cups all-purpose flour

1 teaspoon salt

1 cup olive oil

2 eggplants, ends trimmed,
    cut into ¼-inch-thick rounds

8 slices American cheese

In a large bowl, beat together the eggs, flour, salt, and ½ cup water until smooth.

Heat the olive oil in a large saucepan over medium heat until it sizzles. Dip each eggplant slice into the batter and fry until golden brown, about 3 minutes a side. Transfer the eggplant to a paper towel to drain and cool.

Layer slices of the eggplant with the American cheese and serve.

LUCKY CLAMS WITH PARSLEY AND GARLIC

SERVES 2

At Basille's in Staten Island, we used to call these Clams Luciano, but now we like to call 'em Lucky Clams as a sorta nickname. They were a real popular dish—everybody got Clams Luciano. We had this one guy workin' at the restaurant, and he made these clams the best. He was nuts— used to smoke angel dust seven days a week, this guy. There was a lot of that in Staten Island in the eighties and nineties. We called people like him dust muffins.

Well, this guy—we're not naming names—he was totally shot out of a cannon—was burnt to a crisp. He'd come in to work dusted out of his mind. But the thing was, the guy could cook like you never seen anybody cook. He could have twenty-four burners going at once with a fryer full of chicken cutlets. He was a perfectionist too. He would smoke PCP all day, but if there was a spot of sauce on the edge of one of his plates, forget it. The parsley garnish had to be on the dish just right.

Even though this is a classic restaurant dish, there's not much to it. It's littleneck clams— which are perfect because they're clean and got good meat in 'em—garlic, parsley, olive oil, red pepper flakes, and a lot of sherry cooking wine. We'd serve this as an appetizer, but you could also serve it with pasta. Either way, you gotta have bread on the side for dippin'.

12 littleneck clams, scrubbed

1 tablespoon chopped fresh flat-leaf parsley

2 tablespoons chopped garlic

¼ cup olive oil

½ teaspoon red pepper flakes

Pinch of salt

1 cup sherry cooking wine

2 cups clam juice

1 tablespoon salted butter

5 fresh basil leaves, torn

1 loaf of bread from your
favorite Italian bakery

In a medium saucepan, combine the clams, parsley, garlic, olive oil, red pepper flakes, and salt and cook over medium heat until the garlic browns. Add the sherry and cook for 2 minutes. Add the clam juice and butter and cook until the clams open. Discard any clams that don't open. Finish with fresh basil leaves. Serve with crusty bread.

SALTED AND ROASTED PUMPKIN SEEDS

One of our grandfather's favorite things to do was play solitaire. He used to sit down and really take his time. He'd play until the birds started chirpin' (we hated those freakin' birds). He was real OCD about it too. He had to have his big glass of cold water that said "Dom" on it and, of course, a big pile of pumpkin seeds. Now, he didn't just put all the seeds in his mouth at once like most people. No. Our grandfather would put each shell in his mouth, crack it, and put the seed on the table. Then he'd continue playing solitaire and go to the next seed, put it in his mouth, crack the shell, pull the shell out, take the seed out, and put it on the table. He'd wait until he had like a hundred seeds outta the shell before he actually ate 'em. It was like his reward for workin' so hard to get those seeds out. A lot of times he bought his seeds at the store, but whenever we'd make jack-o'-lanterns for Halloween, he'd just clean off the pumpkin seeds, salt 'em to death, and roast 'em in the oven.

1 pound unshelled pumpkin seeds

2 tablespoons salt

¼ cup olive oil

Preheat the oven to 350°F.

In a medium saucepot, bring just enough water to cover the seeds to a boil. Add the pumpkin seeds and boil for 4 to 5 minutes.

Drain the seeds and spread them evenly on a baking sheet. Coat them with the salt and olive oil and roast for 10 minutes or until they're lightly browned.

GRAHAM CRACKERS AND MILK

SERVES 1

This was something we ate all the time as a snack. We'd take a whole sleeve of Nabisco graham crackers, crack 'em up into a bowl, pour cold milk on top, let the crackers get all mushy, and eat it like it was cereal. This is not somethin' to be taken lightly—it's not some half-assed recipe we cooked up as kids. This is like the best bread puddin' you ever had. If you didn't know what it was and they served it to you at one of Thomas Keller's restaurants, you'd rave about it. No joke.

1 box of graham crackers, preferably Nabisco

1 gallon of whole milk

Crush up one sleeve of the graham crackers into small pieces and put them in a bowl. Pour the milk on top, mash it all together, and eat.

Sal, Fran, and Sal's brother Dominick in Fran's restaurant, Ciao Bella, on Staten Island

5.

STOP EATIN' LIKE A GAVONE

RECIPES ON THE LIGHTER SIDE

OR YOU'LL LOOK LIKE AUNT DEE

When the family got together, there was always somebody who was watchin' their weight. A lotta times there'd be half a grapefruit or melon, some cottage cheese, and crackers instead of bread on the table for when our grandmother, mothers, or aunts were on some kinda yo-yo diet. Our grandmother, she was one of Weight Watchers' first members. If she wasn't cookin' up something for the family, she'd be boilin' some cabbage in a can of tomato soup for herself. Sometimes she'd even allow herself a potato and throw that in there too. Or a hot dog. One cousin even had her jaw wired shut to lose some weight. (Back then it was like their version of Lap-Band surgery.) But the thing was, she'd be puttin' filet mignon and potatoes in a blender and drinkin' it through a straw. She almost killed herself that way, too, but a few years later? She did it again. For the rest of the family, though, losin' a little weight didn't necessarily mean boiled cabbage and steak in a blender. When we or Uncle Tommy or Uncle Greg wanted to knock off a coupla pounds, we'd just make somethin' a little lighter, but no less delicious. As we liked to say, "What's less calories than a sandwich? Half a sandwich."

TORTELLINI AND RED ONIONS

SERVES 4

At Basille's, we'd always use Pastosa fresh pasta—it was the best. You won't find better tortellini than theirs. You could make 'em yourself, but we say let the experts do it. Whenever we made an order of tortellini, we'd only use three-quarters of the bag because otherwise it'd be too much for the dish. So we'd open a bag, use what we needed, then put aside whatever was left over. And every three bags we opened, we'd have enough leftovers for an order. But sometimes, we would cook up those few little tortellini at the bottom of the bag, toss 'em with red onion and kalamata olives from the salad station, then dress the whole thing really simply in olive oil, salt, and pepper with some grated cheese on top. We didn't use any tomato sauce because it gives you agita when you're workin', but you didn't need it because you'd get so much flavor from the other ingredients—the crunch from the red onion and the salt from the olives and the cheese. We never put it on the menu, but we'd always make it whenever we wanted something fast and light. It's just as good cold as it is hot and is perfect to put on the table in the summertime.

Salt

1 pound fresh tortellini, preferably Pastosa

1 red onion, thickly sliced

1 cup kalamata olives, pitted

3 sprigs fresh flat-leaf parsley, finely chopped

½ cup olive oil

Black pepper

½ cup grated pecorino

In a large pot, bring 2 quarts of lightly salted water to a boil. Add the tortellini and cook for 7 minutes, or until tender. Drain the pasta and set it aside in a bowl to cool.

In a large bowl, combine the onion, olives, parsley, and olive oil and season with salt and pepper. Add to the pasta and refrigerate overnight.

When ready to serve, plate the pasta and garnish with the cheese.

BELLA'S NICE SALAD

SERVES 2

Our grandmother, she always said, "I'm gonna make a nice salad." She'd take some iceberg lettuce and onions and toss them with oil and vinegar and a whole lotta salt and pepper. And that was it. That was the salad. It was a staple on our table. Sal's mom, Bella, she put it on the menu at the restaurant. But she used romaine instead of iceberg lettuce, red onion instead of white, and added in some green olives.

½ head iceberg lettuce, roughly chopped

1 ripe medium tomato, cut into 8 wedges

1 small red onion, cut into 8 wedges

1 small cucumber, halved and thickly sliced

6 Sicilian green olives

¼ cup red wine vinegar

½ cup olive oil

Salt and black pepper

Dried oregano

In a large bowl, toss together the lettuce, tomato, onion, cucumber, olives, vinegar, and oil. Season with salt, pepper, and oregano—we recommend salty, 'cause that's how Grandma liked it!

VARIATION:

JOY'S NICE SALAD

Now Fran's mom, Joy, she'd take a meatball outta the pot of sauce and put it right on the salad and eat it like that. She'd shake off most of the sauce first, but there'd still be a little bit that would mix with the oil and vinegar. Then she'd top the whole thing with a little shredded cheese. Or sometimes she'd take the bones outta the soup pot—like the neck bones or the short ribs—take off whatever meat was still on 'em, and put that on the salad. Either way, the heat from the meat wilts the salad a little bit so the texture's a little different. It's really nice.

Prepare Bella's Nice Salad (above), then top the salad with one lightly sauced hot meatball (see Grandma's Meatballs on page 213) and garnish with 1 tablespoon grated pecorino. Serve with a nice piece of crusty Italian bread and eat while listening to Vikki Carr's "It Must Be Him." Boom.

THE PORK STORE "STRING BEAN SALAD"

SERVES 4

This is a very popular dish that you could get in any Staten Island pork store. You know, the places you'd go and buy the same meat they got in the supermarket, but for three times the price—like those sausage pinwheels with parsley and grated cheese? Then they got all kinds of prepared salads that you can buy too. These places thrive in the summertime because anytime you barbecue, you can get anything you need there. Seriously, you can't get out of a pork store in Staten Island without spending at least fifty dollars. It's so stupid, but everybody does it.

This salad, though—Fran's mother would make it herself all the time, especially in the summer because it's really nice served cold. All there was to it was boiling the string beans and potatoes just enough that they cooked, but not too much, so they still had some body on them, then dressin' 'em in some oil and vinegar, salt and pepper.

4 white potatoes, peeled and quartered

1 pound fresh string beans

8 garlic cloves, chopped

¾ cup olive oil

2 tablespoons white vinegar

Put the potatoes in a saucepan, add just enough cold water to cover them, and bring the water to a boil. Reduce the heat to maintain a simmer and cook until the potatoes are tender, 10 to 20 minutes (check every 5 minutes after 10 minutes). Remove the potatoes from the water using a slotted spoon or spider, keeping the water at a boil, and put the potatoes in a colander to drain and cool.

Meanwhile, remove the tips of the string beans and wash them thoroughly—this is a great job for the kids. Place them in the water you used to cook the potatoes and cook for 1 to 2 minutes, until they're tender but still crisp. Drain the green beans and let them cool.

In a large bowl, combine all the ingredients and refrigerate until ready to serve.

EGGPLANT CAPONATA

SERVES 5 TO 6

Caponata, or "gabbonatin," was a real popular dish in our house. It's like a Sicilian version of baba ghanoush, only we don't blend everything together, so it's real fast to make. At the base of it you have eggplant with the skin on, then you add a little bit of celery, some capers and green olives, and then tomato paste or sauce. We'd serve it cold and eat it like a dip the way people do in the Middle East—only with Italian bread. You could also do our grandfather proud and make this with Pickled Eggplant (page 102).

1 cup white vinegar

¼ cup sugar

1 cup olive oil

2 medium eggplants, ends trimmed, diced into 1-inch cubes

1 large onion, diced

4 stalks celery, diced

2 garlic cloves, finely chopped

1 (16-ounce) can tomato sauce, or 2 cups Marinara Sauce (page 142)

½ cup kalamata olives, pitted

½ cup drained capers

¼ cup pignoli nuts

1 loaf Italian bread, for serving

Provolone cheese, for serving

In a large saucepan, bring the vinegar to a boil over high heat. Add the sugar and continue boiling until the mixture has reduced by about half. Remove from the heat.

In a large sauté pan, heat the olive oil over medium-high heat. Add the eggplant, onion, celery, and garlic and sauté until browned and tender. Add the tomato sauce and reduced vinegar mixture and simmer for 30 minutes. Remove the mixture from the heat and set it aside to cool. Stir in the olives, capers, and pignoli nuts.

Serve the caponata at room temperature with crispy Italian bread and pieces of provolone.

PICKLED EGGPLANT

MAKES 8 (16-OUNCE) BALL JARS

Whenever our grandfather wasn't cooking, he'd be bottling sauce and makin' bread crumbs and, best of all, picklin' eggplant. And after he moved to Florida and retired, he really went nuts. When he died, he left an entire garage packed to the ceiling with it. You woulda thought he had a factory, there was so much. No kidding, we were eatin' that eggplant ten years after that. That was his legacy, all that friggin' eggplant. And it was delicious—real tangy and sour, all vinegar. The best way to describe the flavor would be Extreme Pickle. We'd eat it mixed into Eggplant Caponata (page 101), with olives and sopressata on Italian bread, or plain—right outta the jar. When we were sixteen, we went to visit him out in Florida. We'd just gotten our licenses, which is pretty much the coolest thing in the world to a teenager, and we'd rented a Cutlass, the International Series. It was a nice car, like a muscle car. So we go to our grandfather's house, went on his boat, and so on. When we left, of course he gave us a coupla jars of eggplant. So we're drivin' across Florida to get back to the airport, which was four or five hours away, and at one point, Fran turns to Sal and says, "Wanna eat the eggplant?" So we set up the jar in the center console and start eatin' it with our fingers, grease gettin' all over the seats, the steerin' wheel, our pants. It was that good.

One of the secrets to the pickled eggplant was that it never touched heat, so it never got all mushade. And before our grandfather pickled it, he'd submerge the eggplant in water and salt—"to take the agita out of it," he'd say. Then it would get bottled with vinegar, olive oil, red pepper flakes, salt, and garlic. And that was it.

½ pound (¾ cup) salt

4 large eggplants, ends trimmed,
   cut into ¼-inch-thick rounds

3 cups white vinegar

1 cup olive oil

6 garlic cloves

1 teaspoon black pepper

2 tablespoons red pepper flakes

Fill a large pot, bowl, or tub with enough water to completely cover the eggplant. Add salt, using enough to make the water taste salty, like seawater. Put the eggplant in the water and make sure it stays submerged by weighting it down with a pot lid or plate. Cover the container and let it sit overnight. Periodically check to see if the water has turned brown. When it has, drain off the water and replace it with clean, salted water.

The next day, transfer the eggplant to a large bowl and add the vinegar, olive oil, garlic cloves, 2 teaspoons of salt, the black pepper, and the red pepper flakes.

To sterilize your jars for storage, bring a large pot of water to a boil. Submerge the open jars and lids and boil for five minutes. Dry out the jars and fill them with the pickled eggplant and brine. Close the jars and return them to the pot of boiling water. Boil the jars for another 5 minutes to create a vacuum seal. The pickles should be ready for eating in 10 to 14 days.

Grandpa Dominick (second from right) with his cousins in Italy.

ORANGE SALAD

SERVES 1 TO 2

Our grandfather was always making this as a light snack. He'd peel the oranges; toss 'em with oil, salt, and pepper; and eat it just like that.

We have two versions of this salad.

Grandpa made it simple:

2 oranges, peeled and segmented
Olive oil
Salt and black pepper

Combine the ingredients in a bowl and serve.

In the restaurant, we made it a little more fancy:

2 oranges, peeled and segmented
1 bag mesclun lettuce mix
1 tomato, cut into 8 wedges
1 stalk celery, sliced
4 walnuts, toasted and crushed
¼ red onion, sliced
½ cup red wine vinegar
½ cup olive oil
Salt and black pepper

Combine the ingredients in a bowl and shake it like a Polaroid picture.

CAVOLO RICCIO

SERVES 4

Everybody's obsessed with kale now, so we figured we'd throw in a nice recipe for it.

2 bunches kale, stems removed,
  leaves roughly chopped

¼ cup olive oil

2 garlic cloves, minced

2½ cups Cooked Sauce (page 141)

3 tablespoons drained salted capers

1 (10-ounce) jar Manzanilla olives, sliced

1½ cups chopped pecorino

Bring a large pot of water to a boil. Add the kale and cook until tender, 3 to 4 minutes. Drain and set aside.

In a separate large saucepot, heat the olive oil over medium heat. Add the garlic and cook until it browns. Add the sauce, capers, and olives and cook for 20 minutes. Stir in the kale and cheese, cook for a few minutes more so everything comes together, and serve.

SCUNGILLI SALAD WITH KALAMATA OLIVES

SERVES 2

We remember our grandfather having stacks of LaMonica scungilli, or sliced conch, in the pantry. He loved the stuff, and from a very early age we learned that canned scungilli blew fresh scungilli outta the water. You just couldn't get the same product out of the fresh. The LaMonica brand was all we knew, and it was always so tender. And since it was ready to eat, you didn't need to do much to it. Our grandfather would cook it up in a little tomato sauce and serve it over pasta, nice and simple, or he'd make this dish. He'd add some olive oil, lemon juice, maybe some vinegar, a little bit of parsley and oregano, throw some olives and red onion on it, then toss it like a salad and serve it cold. It was great for the summertime, or just when you needed somethin' fast.

1 (29-ounce) can La Monica scungilli

8 kalamata olives, pitted

½ cup sliced red onion

1 stalk celery, sliced

1 garlic clove, minced

Juice of ½ lemon

2 sprigs fresh flat-leaf parsley, chopped

¼ cup olive oil

2 tablespoons white vinegar

1 teaspoon dried oregano

1 lemon, cut into wedges, for serving

Drain the scungilli and put it in a bowl. Add the remaining ingredients, except the lemon wedges, and toss to combine. Cover and refrigerate until ready to eat. Serve the salad chilled, with a garnish of lemon wedges.

TOMATO AND ONION SALAD

SERVES 4 TO 6

This dish is really a summertime thing because tomatoes suck the rest of the year. Anytime you're gonna barbecue or you're doin' chicken or steak, this would be the side. Or even just with Italian bread to sop up all the juices that are left over from the tomatoes and onions marinatin', it's phenomenal. Like a delicious dressing. The longer this salad sits, the better it gets. We can picture our grandma Connie sittin' in her Florida sunroom eatin' this with some bread. The dressing was even better when she made it because she made everything so salty.

4 heirloom tomatoes, cut into 8 wedges

1 white onion, cut into 8 wedges

½ cup extra-virgin olive oil

2 teaspoons salt

1 teaspoon black pepper

1 teaspoon dried oregano

In a large bowl, toss the ingredients together. Serve chilled.

Grandma Connie

ITALIAN TUNA SALAD

SERVES 1

This was our grandfather's thing, and it's what you ate in our house if you had a tuna fish sandwich. It wasn't your typical tuna with mayo on Wonder Bread. Instead, it was canned dark Italian tuna tossed with olive oil, salt, pepper, and white onions. To him, it was diet food because it didn't have any cheese or mayo. He'd eat it on bread, but you could serve it over some greens instead.

1 (5-ounce) can dark Italian tuna packed in olive oil

¼ white onion, diced

6 black olives, pitted and sliced

2 tablespoons olive oil

1 tablespoon red wine vinegar

Salt and black pepper

1 loaf crusty Italian bread, halved lengthwise, or 1 head iceberg lettuce

½ tomato, sliced

Drain the tuna and put it in a medium bowl. Add the onion, olives, olive oil, and vinegar and toss to combine. Season with salt and pepper to taste. Heap the mixture on the bread or on some lettuce, and top with the tomato slices.

CAULIFLOWER AND MACARONI, MINUS THE MACARONI

SERVES 4

Whenever Fran's on one of his yo-yo diets, he cooks up this version of Cauliflower and Macaroni (page 149). It's great because you could eat a whole head of cauliflower and still only have like 40 calories, but it sits in your stomach like a rock. And when you eat it hot with tomato sauce and grated cheese and black pepper, you feel like you're eatin' macaroni.

1 recipe Cauliflower and Macaroni (page 149), but forget the macaroni

PEPPERS AND EGG WHITES

SERVES 1 OR 2

Believe it or not, there was a point in our lives when we were actually athletic-lookin'. And when we were in good shape, we were always tryin' to look jacked. One of the things in the restaurant that was good protein was egg whites. Or as we like to say, "Save the yolks for Rocky!" We'd cook the whites up with a little olive oil and some peppers and onions.

3 tablespoons olive oil

½ green bell pepper, seeded
   and sliced lengthwise

6 large egg whites

1 tablespoon grated pecorino

Salt and black pepper

In a medium nonstick frying pan, heat the olive oil over medium heat. Add the bell peppers and sauté for about 3 minutes, or until your neighbors start to smell it.

When the peppers are tender, reduce the heat to low and add the egg whites to the pan. Use a spatula to mix in the cheese and salt and pepper to taste, and cook until the eggs are fluffy and just cooked. Eat it just like it is—save the bread and bread crumbs for fat boys!

UNCLE PUDGIE'S CHICKEN

(CHICKEN WITH BREAD CRUMBS)

SERVES 4 TO 6

Our moms had three brothers: Tommy, Greg, and Vincent (Vinnie, or Pudgie, as we all called him), and they all boxed. Uncle Tommy was really good, Uncle Greg was really good, but Uncle Pudgie? He always got beat up. Our grandmother hated goin' to his fights because he was always losin', but he had a lotta heart and kept at it. He was always tryin' to keep healthy, too, so he liked to cook chicken, and this was his favorite way to do it because it wasn't fried. It's sorta like Shake 'n Bake, where you roll the chicken in seasoned Dry Bread Crumbs (page 79) and roast it at a really low temperature so it stays all moist and tender and keeps all its flavor.

1 cup olive oil, plus more for the pan

2 cups Dry Bread Crumbs (page 79)

4 chicken thighs

4 chicken legs

4 chicken wings

4 chicken breasts

Preheat the oven to 325°F.

Grease a rimmed baking sheet with about 1 tablespoon olive oil.

Pour the 1 cup olive oil into a bowl. Put the bread crumbs in a separate shallow bowl. Use a paper towel to pat the chicken pieces dry. Dip each piece into the oil, then dredge it in the bread crumbs, making sure it's well coated. Lay the breaded chicken pieces in the prepared pan and bake until browned, about 2 hours.

BROILED LEGS AND THIGHS WITH LEMON

SERVES 2

Our grandmother, she could sit there all day and eat chicken on the bone with lemon and salt. But instead of cooking it all together like most normal people, she'd broil the chicken first, then she'd dress each individual piece as she ate it. First a squeeze of lemon, and then the salt. Jesus, the salt. Anything she ate, she salted to death. Even those little Kirby cucumber pickles—she'd salt 'em. It didn't matter if Sal's mom was cookin' or Fran's mom was cookin' or we were out at a restaurant—before she even tasted something, she'd be reachin' for the saltshaker. So anyways, that's how she ate her chicken, like it was an activity or somethin'. We never really knew why she did it that way, but after we started makin' this dish ourselves, we realized she was onto something: When you give the chicken a squeeze of lemon at the very end, it doesn't have a chance to drip off, so you get all that pungent, delicious flavor mixed with the chicken's juices, all in one shot.

4 chicken legs

4 chicken thighs

1 lemon, cut into wedges

Salt and black pepper

Preheat the oven to broil, or to 450°F.

Arrange the chicken pieces on a baking sheet and cook until well done, about 1½ hours.

Finish by squeezing the lemon over the chicken and seasoning generously with salt and pepper.

Clockwise from top left: Sal's father, Vito, making pizza;
Uncle Tommy and Vito; Vito, making pizza; Fran's brother
Vincent with Sal

6.

—WHAT WE DO—
• PIZZA •

Pizza is what we grew up doin' our entire lives. It's what put clothes on our backs. It's what got us out of speeding tickets. It's what made us cool in the neighborhood. It made us who we are today. It *made us*, period. In Staten Island, people didn't care whose trust fund was bigger or if you were a Kardashian—if you had a good pizzeria, you were a somebody. Well, if we had to crown a King of Pizza in Staten Island, that would have to be Sal's father, Vito. He opened the first Basille's restaurant in 1988. Our family owned tons of pizzerias and hero shops and bakeries and other restaurants before that, but his was the biggest success, the family's big splash. Back then, there was no Internet or Yelp or bloggers or stuff like that—it was all word of mouth. If you were good, that was street cred.

And let us tell you, Vito was *good*. We were the pizzeria everybody talked about. There was always a wait for tables—Friday and Saturday nights, you had to wait an hour and a half, maybe two hours just to get in. Why? Basille's raised the bar for what you could get in a pizzeria. It wasn't just cheese and sausage and pepperoni. We made one of the first broccoli rabe pies with garlic and red pepper flakes and olive oil. People had never seen that before! Then there was the *sfinguini* with anchovies, onions, bread crumbs, and sauce. And all the ingredients were good. We weren't usin' mushrooms outta the can; we'd be in the back, choppin' 'em up, fryin' 'em, seasonin' 'em, and puttin' 'em down on the pizzas. They were the best mushrooms you ever ate. (Check out Fast Mushrooms, page 70).

What also set Vito apart from the competition was that he made his dough by hand. Back then, you could buy a giant mixer with different attachments to make dough and shred cheese, but they were big money. And because most people were only chargin' like a dollar for a slice, it wasn't enough to buy fancy machinery. So Vito, he'd put the flour, the water, the yeast—everythin'—in a big wooden box and mix it all on his own. Do you know what a job that is? Our uncle Tommy, who worked alongside Vito for thirty years, his hands are made out of Teflon now. He's a seventy-year-old man and can take the Yellow Pages and rip 'em in half. It's an amazing grip this man has. He always says we could do the same thing if we were mixin' three boxes of dough by hand a day for that many years.

The other thing Vito would do was take his balls of mozzarella and instead of shreddin' 'em, he'd cut 'em into blocks with a dough cutter. Then he'd put the cheese down first and the sauce on top of that—the same way we do it now. No one in Staten Island was doin' it that way then, and no one we know does it now. But think about it—you get a steamin' hot piece outta the oven, pick it up, and what happens? The cheese slides right off. When you cook it our way—the way Vito taught us—the cheese melts into the dough. It's a totally different product. You can take the same cheese and the same sauce and prepare it these two ways and end up with two completely different pies. The taste might be similar, but the mouthfeel and texture won't be. So puttin' the cheese on first and then the sauce was what made Basille's different; it's what gave us our edge. Everybody else was doin' it the same way, takin' the easy way out—just takin' a ladle of sauce and smooshin' it around. With our way, you gotta control the ladle, hold it like you're holdin' a paintbrush. Whenever we got new hires, the hardest thing to teach 'em was puttin' on the sauce. They'd be used to hittin' the dough with the sauce real fast and then sprinklin' on the cheese. Now they had to be careful, do it more gingerly. The distribution of the sauce has to be perfectly even over the pie.

When we opened Artichoke, we wanted to raise the bar even higher. You could even say we went overboard, but for us, it was just makin' pizza the way we wanted to eat it. So we started adding the best ingredients to every single pie—Parmigiano-Reggiano and olive oil and basil. In Staten Island, we couldn't get away with that because people couldn't afford what we'd have to charge just to break even for those ingredients. But our philosophy was, and continues to be, "Let's make everything the best we can and charge for it." We went after people who wanted the best. People who wanted something different and better. And if not, there's five other pizzerias around the block they can go to instead.

....

The whole world likes pizza. But in New York City, we have a love affair with it. Italian-American pizza as we know it was born here. New York City is the "slice joint" capital of the world, but if you can't make it out to the Big Apple, we're gonna show you how to make it right in your own kitchen.

First, let's talk about your oven. What gives New York–style pizza its signature crispy crust is the deck ovens that we use. Deck ovens have thick stones, which we cook the pies directly on. These stones retain a lot of heat and give our crusts that unbeatable bottom. To convert your home oven, you're gonna need a pizza stone. Don't have one? You can use quarry tiles. Go to Home Depot, buy a box of quarry tiles, set your oven rack all the way to the bottom, and lay your stone or quarry tile over the rack. The stone or tiles need to be heated all the way through before you put your pizza on them; otherwise, you'll end up with a cooked top and a soggy bottom. Turn your oven up as high as it goes—we're talking 550 to 600°F—and let it preheat for at least an hour.

Once you've got your oven ready, you can start preparing the dough. One of the other key ingredients to creating a real New York City pizza is making the dough with real New York City tap water. New York City tap water is by far the best-tasting tap water in the world. It's a fact—google it. But if you're not in New York City, don't worry: You can use bottled Poland Spring water, which, in our opinion, is a close second when talking about great-tasting water. It's just as soft and works wonders with dough. If you can't get Poland Spring, go with Dasani.

To make the dough, you'll need:

1 tablespoon instant dry yeast

2½ teaspoons salt

¼ cup olive oil, plus more for the bowl

1 cup warm water

3½ cups high-gluten flour

All-purpose flour for coating
    your peel and work surface

In a large bowl, combine the yeast, salt, oil, and water. (The salt is gonna give it great taste and color and the oil provides the great texture.) Add the flour and mix it in by hand until the mixture forms a ball and looks smooth. Take the dough out of the bowl, grease the bowl with a little oil, then place the dough ball back in the bowl (the oil will keep it from sticking). Cover the bowl with a dishtowel or something else that's not airtight that will

allow the dough to breathe. Set it aside for an hour at room temperature; it should double in size.

While the dough is proofing, get your sauce and toppings ready. As you'll see in chapter 7 on sauces, New York–style pizza sauce is very simple: All there is to it is tomatoes, salt, and olive oil. And it isn't cooked ahead of time; instead, it cooks on the pie when it goes into the oven. That's it, plain and simple. For the full recipe, see page 143.

Now you're going to need what we call a peel—a wide, flat wooden "shovel"—to get your pie into the oven. If you don't have one, that's okay; you can use the top of any pizza box or any other piece of cardboard that's at least 16 by 16 inches. First, flour your peel (or your cardboard). On a floured work surface, start stretching your dough, pressing down from the outside and working your way into the middle. Try not to take all of the air out of it. Once it's flattened, pick it up and gently toss it back and forth. Try not to let the center get thin. It's important that the dough is even. Stretch it into a roughly 16-inch circle, then put it on the floured peel.

Now, over the top of your dough, sprinkle some cheese, spread your sauce, and add any other toppings. Carefully slide the pizza onto your pizza stone or tiles and let it cook for 12 to 15 minutes, until it looks like all the cheese has melted and started to brown. While it's cooking, jump in your car, drive in reverse to the nearest store that sells Coca-Cola, run in, and yell, "Yo! Where's the Coca-Cola at?" Grab your bottle, pay the guy, get in your car, and punch it home while blasting Frank Sinatra's "New York, New York." Take the pizza out of the oven, let it cool, get a pizza cutter, cut it up, sprinkle on the Parmigiano-Reggiano, drizzle on some olive oil, pour some Coke over ice ('cause the ice cuts the Coke), and enjoy. See that? We just saved you a trip to New York. But when you do come to New York, make sure you come to Artichoke Pizza and ask for Fran and Sal.

SICILIAN PIZZA

SERVES 4

Our moms made Sicilian pizza at the restaurant, but the way we wanted to make it at our place was just like our great-grandfather used to do it in his own oven. He had an apartment in Brooklyn Heights—or whateva they're callin' it these days—and when he made this pizza, he would always burn the life out of it. That was part of the secret—and now it's one of our most popular slices.

The dough cooks twice—the first time, it sorta fries in all the oil you put in the pan, and it becomes a sponge for the grease. Then you add two different types of "muzzarell": Polly-O and fresh. Polly-O is low-moisture and high-butterfat. It's greasy—let's just put it that way. But it's not like a lot of other muzzarells that get like bubblegum when you cook 'em. Polly-O doesn't do that. The cheese gets topped with our Pizza Sauce (page 143) and a huge handful of pecorino, then goes back in the oven, where we cook it to death. That way you get a nice slice that doesn't fall apart, and all the flavors are really melded together. It's not all loose and mushade.

Our first Artichoke Pizza had been open maybe two weeks when a woman came in askin' if we were the owners. She told us that her mother had brought home a Sicilian pie the other day and that when she ate it, she started to cry. It reminded her of her grandmother, who used to make it that way in her house. You can't get a product like that if you're takin' shortcuts. So maybe this recipe is a little bit of a pain in the ass—tryin' to stretch the dough to fit the pan while it's fightin' ya, cookin' it twice, all that oil splashin' around, and all that cheese—but it makes an amazing pie.

For the Sicilian Dough:

2½ teaspoons salt

1 tablespoon dry yeast

¼ cup warm water

¼ cup olive oil, plus more for the bowl

3½ cups all-purpose flour

For the Pizza:

Olive oil

All-purpose flour, for dusting

1 recipe Pizza Sauce (page 143)

½ pound Polly-O whole-milk mozzarella, cut or torn into 1-inch pieces

2 ounces fresh mozzarella, cut or torn into 1-inch pieces

¼ cup grated pecorino

20 fresh basil leaves, torn in half

¼ cup grated Parmigiano-Reggiano

CONTINUED

MAKE THE SICILIAN DOUGH:

In a large bowl, combine the salt, yeast, and water. Mix with a spoon, then add the olive oil and flour and mix until the ingredients form a ball and look smooth. Remove the dough ball from the bowl, coat the bowl with oil, and put the dough back in the bowl to proof. Cover the bowl with a dishtowel or something else that's not airtight that will allow the dough to breathe. Set it aside for an hour. The dough should double in size.

MAKE THE PIZZA:

Preheat the oven to 500°F. Coat a 16 x 11-inch roasting pan or baking dish with 1 cup olive oil.

Turn out the dough onto a floured surface. Gently stretch it, pressing down from the outside and working your way toward the middle. Try not to take all the air out of the dough. Once it's flattened, place it in the prepared baking dish and gently pull it to fit the shape of the dish. Take a knife and poke as many holes as you can through the dough. (If it's an aluminum roasting pan, make sure you don't poke any holes through the pan!)

Brush some olive oil on top of the dough and top with ¼ cup of the tomato sauce. Bake for about 5 minutes, until the dough gets golden brown on top. Remove from the oven and spread the mozzarella on top as evenly as possible. Then spread the remaining sauce to cover the mozzarella. Sprinkle the pecorino evenly over the top and return the pizza to the oven for 12 minutes more, or until the cheese is golden brown. Remove from the oven, top with the basil and Parmigiano-Reggiano, and serve hot.

HOMEMADE WINE

Our great-grandfather Gregory used to make homemade wine. He'd store it in empty Coca-Cola bottles, and because he didn't have a lot of space in his little Red Hook apartment, he'd leave 'em out on the counter to ferment. Fran remembers goin' over to Grandpa Gregory's house one day and drinkin' a bottle of soda with his Sicilian pizza. Fran had to have been four or five at the time, but he remembers—swear to God—that he could tell the soda tasted funny. Eventually his father figured out it was the wine!

❧

MARGHERITA PIZZA

SERVES 4

People were always comin' into Basille's and asking for a "regular pie." After a while, we just started callin' it a Margherita because it was fashionable. Most Margherita pies are the Neapolitan style—fresh mozzarella, plum tomatoes, olive oil, and basil. No grated cheese or the American-style Polly-O mozzarella that we love so much at Artichoke. So when we opened our shop, we combined the traditional Margherita with our Staten Island–style pie. We blend Polly-O mozzarella with fresh mozzarella and add some Parmigiano-Reggiano and pecorino. If you talk to a pizza buff, they'll argue that it's not a real Margherita. But who ever wrote the book on that anyway?

To get the perfect Margherita pizza, follow our instructions on pages 120–23 (Making New York Pizzeria–Quality Pizza at Home). As for the cheese, you'll need to find real whole-milk mozzarella, preferably Polly-O (the good stuff). You're also going to need fresh mozzarella, Parmigiano-Reggiano, and pecorino.

1 recipe Pizza Dough (pages 120–23),
  proofed and prepped

10 ounces whole-milk mozzarella,
  preferably Polly-O (just buy a pound and
  use what you use), cut into 1-inch cubes

1 recipe Pizza Sauce (page 143)

¼ cup grated pecorino

1 ball fresh mozzarella, cut or
  torn into 1-inch pieces

½ cup grated Parmigiano-Reggiano

20 fresh basil leaves, torn in half

Olive oil, for drizzling

Spread the dough into a round on your peel. Distribute the cubed mozzarella evenly over the dough and spread two 6-ounce ladlefuls of the sauce over the cheese. Start from the edge and create a bull's-eye right up to the middle. Try to distribute it as evenly as possible. Sprinkle the pecorino evenly over the sauce, and arrange the fresh mozzarella on top of that. Bake for 12 to 15 minutes, until it looks like all the cheese has melted and started to brown. Finish with the basil, the Parmigiano-Reggiano, and a drizzle of olive oil.

EGGPLANT PIZZA WITH SICILIAN CRUST

SERVES 4

This was another really popular pie at Basille's. But because it was so popular, we had to change the way we made the eggplant. We couldn't fry it to order because it was a real busy restaurant and the kitchen was small. And we couldn't fry it in advance and put it in the fridge because it would get all mushade and stick together like a mess. We figured out that when you egged it, breaded it, and baked it, you could keep it for a few hours and it wouldn't get all messed up. We'd bang out a signature square Sicilian crust, put down some chopped mozzarella and two big ladles of Cooked Sauce (page 141), and pile on the eggplant. Then we added more sauce, some pecorino, more chopped mozzarella, and a layer of sliced fresh mozzarella on top so it would brown. It was like gettin' a giant tray of eggplant parm. So friggin' good. It's also amazing when you have leftovers that you heat back up in the oven.

3 large eggs

1 cup whole milk

2 cups Dry Bread Crumbs (page 79)

1 eggplant, peeled and cut into ¼-inch-thick rounds

1 cup olive oil, plus more as needed

1 recipe Sicilian Dough (page 125), proofed and prepared

All-purpose flour, for dusting

3 cups Cooked Sauce (page 141)

½ pound whole-milk mozzarella, preferably Polly-O, cut or torn into 1-inch pieces

¼ cup grated pecorino, plus more as needed

Preheat the oven to 450°F.

In a medium bowl, beat together the eggs and milk. Place the bread crumbs in a separate shallow bowl.

Soak the eggplant slices in the egg mixture, then dredge them in the bread crumbs until well coated.

Coat a rimmed baking sheet with a thin layer of olive oil and spread the breaded eggplant rounds in one layer on the pan. Generously drizzle olive oil on top. Bake the eggplant for 15 minutes, or until golden brown. Remove the pan from the oven and raise the oven heat to 500°F.

CONTINUED

Pour the 1 cup olive oil into a 16 x 11-inch roasting pan or baking dish.

Turn out the dough onto a floured surface. Gently stretch it, pressing down from the outside and working your way toward the middle. Try not to take all the air out of the dough. Once it's flattened, place it in the prepared baking dish and gently pull it to fit the shape of the dish. Take a knife and poke as many holes as you can through the dough. (If it's an aluminum roasting pan, make sure you don't poke any holes through the pan!)

Brush some olive oil on the dough and spread ¼ cup of the tomato sauce on top. Bake for about 5 minutes, until the dough gets golden brown on top. Remove the pan from the oven and distribute the mozzarella as evenly as possible over the dough. Spread some sauce to cover the mozzarella. Cover that with the pecorino and eggplant, then add more sauce and mozzarella on top. Bake for 12 minutes more, or until the cheese is golden brown. Remove from the oven, top with additional pecorino, and serve hot.

....

STATEN ISLAND PIE

SERVES 4

There was a place on the North Shore of Staten Island called Jimmy Max. Before Basille's opened, it was the pizzeria we grew up on. We'd always order the same pie there—meatballs, onions, and ricotta. It was their house specialty. But then people started comin' in to Basille's and askin' us to make it. So when we opened a new Artichoke in Chelsea, we added it to our menu as an ode to our Staten Island roots. We do it with our Cooked Sauce (page 141), Grandma's Meatballs (page 213), red onion, and big globs of ricotta—every slice has a couple of dollops.

1 recipe Pizza Dough (pages 120-23), proofed and prepped

3 cups Cooked Sauce (page 141)

½ pound whole-milk mozzarella, preferably Polly-O, cut into 1-inch cubes

8 Grandma's Meatballs (page 213)

1 red onion, thinly sliced

1 cup ricotta

½ cup grated pecorino

Preheat the oven to 500°F.

Spread the dough into a round on your peel. Ladle about half the sauce onto the dough and spread it evenly. Arrange the mozzarella evenly over the pie. Next, smash the meatballs and crumble them all over the pizza. Spread the red onion over the top and use a tablespoon to dollop the ricotta cheese all over. Finish by sprinkling some of the pecorino over the top, and then cook for 15 minutes, or until the cheese is golden and bubbling. When the pizza is ready, remove it from the oven and sprinkle it again with a generous amount of the pecorino. Serve hot.

BROCCOLI RABE PIZZA

When we think of a broccoli rabe pie, we think of Vito (see page 118).

¼ cup plus 2 teaspoons salt

2 bunches broccoli rabe, bottom inch of the
    stems removed and the rest cut into roughly
    2-inch pieces

3 tablespoons chopped garlic

¼ cup olive oil

1 teaspoon black pepper

1 teaspoon red pepper flakes

1 recipe Pizza Dough (pages 120–23),
    proofed and prepped

10 ounces whole-milk mozzarella, preferably
    Polly-O (just buy a pound and use what
    you use), cut into 1-inch cubes

1 recipe Pizza Sauce (page 143)

Preheat the oven to 500°F.

Bring a large pot of water to a rolling boil and add the ¼ cup salt. Add the broccoli rabe and blanch for 1 to 2 minutes, or until just tender. Drain the broccoli rabe and transfer it to a large bowl. Toss it with the garlic, olive oil, remaining 2 teaspoons salt, black pepper, and red pepper flakes.

Spread the dough into a round on your peel. Distribute the cubed mozzarella evenly over the dough and spread two 6-ounce ladlefuls of sauce over the cheese. Start from the edge and create a bull's-eye right up to the middle. Try to distribute it as evenly as possible. Sprinkle the broccoli rabe mixture evenly over the sauce. Bake for 12 to 15 minutes, until it looks like all the cheese has melted and started to brown.

SFINGUINI

This pie has Cooked Sauce (page 141) in a Sicilian crust topped with anchovy, onion, grated cheese, and bread crumbs. The real way to make this (in Italy) might be to do it without sauce and just sprinkle everything with bread crumbs, but we think this is much more delicious. Whoever said Italians know everything?

1 cup olive oil, plus more as needed

1 recipe Sicilian Dough (page 125), proofed and prepped

All-purpose flour, for dusting

1¾ cups Cooked Sauce (page 141)

1 white onion, chopped

16 anchovies

2 cups Dry Bread Crumbs (page 79)

½ cup grated pecorino

Preheat the oven to 500°F. Grease a 16 x 11-inch roasting pan or baking dish with olive oil.

Turn out the dough onto a floured surface. Gently stretch it, pressing down from the outside and working your way toward the middle. Try not to take all the air out of the dough. Once it's flattened, place it in the prepared baking dish and gently pull it to fit the shape of the dish. Take a knife and poke as many holes as you can through the dough. (If it's an aluminum roasting pan, make sure you don't poke any holes through the pan!)

Brush some olive oil on the dough and spread ¼ cup of the tomato sauce on top. Bake for about 5 minutes, until the dough gets golden brown on top. Remove from the oven, leaving the oven on, and distribute the onion, anchovies, and bread crumbs on top as evenly as possible. Spread the remaining sauce over the toppings to cover. Finish with the pecorino. Bake for 12 minutes more, or until the cheese is golden brown.

Uncle Tommy with Sal's brother Dominick

7.

S auce was everything in our house. It was the glue that brought all our meals together. It was the stuff that dreams were made of. But don't be fooled—tomato sauce isn't as simple as you think. Don't go thinkin' that the sauce you put on your pizza is the same sauce you'd pour over your pasta. There's an order to these things. Each sauce has its own special purpose. Cooked Sauce (page 141) is what you make on Sunday. It's a labor of love, cooked slow with pork neck bones and short rib bones, and it has all kinds of crazy rich flavor. That's what you'd use if you wanted spaghetti and meatballs, chicken parm, or tortellini. Marinara, on the other hand, means "fast." It's a sauce you make quick, with just a little bit of wine and some parsley. We use it if somebody wants a sauce that's a little tangier, maybe as a dipping sauce or for a side of linguine. After that comes Pizza Sauce (page 143). That's not cooked at all—it's just plum tomatoes with a little olive oil and salt. Seriously, real New York City pizzerias don't add any garlic, pepper, or oregano; and sauce doesn't cook until the pie goes into the oven. Of course, some of our pies use other sauces for a little somethin' extra-special, but if you're gonna go traditional, then it's gonna be uncooked, simple sauce. Last, you got Seafood Fra Diavolo Sauce (page 143). It's almost the same as marinara, but also has clams and mussels cooked into it. It's perfect for things like Shrimp Marinara (page 193).

Most of these recipes make a lot of sauce. That's because we're normally cookin' for at least twenty people. We realize you're probably not doin' that at home, but if you're gonna go through the trouble of makin' sauce, you might as well make a whole bunch. Just store it in the freezer and it'll stay good forever. All you have to do is leave it out at room temperature to defrost, then heat it up, and you got fresh sauce.

....

Grandma Connie making a pot of sauce

COOKED SAUCE

MAKES ABOUT 1½ GALLONS (24 CUPS)

2½ Spanish white onions, finely chopped

1¾ cups olive oil

¼ cup salt

2 tablespoons black pepper

3 beef short rib bones

3 pork neck bones

4 quarts canned peeled tomatoes, preferably
   Tuttorosso or Redpack

1 (56-ounce) can tomato puree, preferably Suzy Bell

In a large saucepot, combine the onions, olive oil, salt, and pepper and cook over medium heat until the onions brown.

Add the bones and turn the heat down to low. Allow the bones to render for about 15 minutes while stirring occasionally.

In a large bowl, crush the peeled tomatoes by hand until they have a chunky consistency. Add the crushed tomatoes and tomato puree to the pot and simmer for 2 hours, stirring every 5 minutes. Like we said, it's a labor of love.

MARINARA SAUCE

MAKES ABOUT 1½ GALLONS (24 CUPS)

2½ Spanish white onions,
  finely chopped

1¾ cups olive oil

¼ cup chopped garlic

2 tablespoons red pepper flakes

1¾ cups white wine, preferably Chardonnay

4 quarts peeled tomatoes, preferably
  Tuttorosso or Redpack

1 (56-ounce) can tomato puree,
  preferably Suzy Bell

1 bunch fresh flat-leaf parsley,
  leaves and stems chopped

1 tablespoon dried oregano

¼ cup salt

2 tablespoons black pepper

20 fresh basil leaves

In a large saucepot, combine the onions and olive oil and cook over medium heat until the onions brown. Add the garlic and red pepper flakes and stir until the garlic has browned.

Add the white wine and let it cook for 3 minutes.

Meanwhile, in a large bowl, smash the peeled tomatoes by hand until they reach a chunky consistency.

Add the crushed tomatoes and tomato puree to the pot. Season with the parsley, oregano, salt, and pepper.

Cook over low heat for 1 hour, and finish with torn basil leaves before serving.

PIZZA SAUCE

MAKES ABOUT 2½ CUPS

Get a can of peeled Italian plum tomatoes—preferably Tuttorosso or Redpack, but California tomatoes are just as good. For one pizza, use a 20-ounce can. Pour the tomatoes into a bowl and smash them with your hands until they have the consistency of a chunky sauce. Add 3 pinches of salt and ¼ cup olive oil. That's it, plain and simple.

....

SEAFOOD FRA DIAVOLO SAUCE

MAKES ABOUT 1½ GALLONS (24 CUPS)

4 quarts canned peeled tomatoes, preferably Tuttorosso or Redpack

1¾ cups olive oil

½ cup chopped garlic

¼ cup red pepper flakes

1 bunch fresh flat-leaf parsley, leaves and stems chopped

4 chowder (or quahog) clams, scrubbed

8 mussels, scrubbed and debearded

2 cups white wine, preferably Chardonnay

3¾ cups clam juice

¼ cup salt

2 tablespoons black pepper

20 fresh basil leaves, torn

In a large bowl, smash the tomatoes by hand until they reach a chunky consistency. Set aside.

In a large saucepot, combine the olive oil, garlic, red pepper flakes, parsley, clams, and mussels and cook over low heat until the garlic browns.

Add the white wine and cook for 3 minutes more. Add the clam juice.

Add the tomatoes, salt, and black pepper and cook for 1½ hours. Finish the sauce with the basil before serving.

Front: Grandpa Dominick and Grandma Connie;
back: Fran with Sal's brother Dominick

Clockwise from left: Sal's brothers Vincent and Dominick,
Sal, and Grandma Connie

8

GET IN THE HOUSE!
WEEKNIGHT SUPPERS

G rowin' up, our moms worked, which meant that weeknight suppers had to be fast. It was usually just a simple one-pot dish that didn't take more than an hour to prepare, maybe with a coupla sides. Or if our moms were workin' late, a lotta nights we'd eat at our grandma and grandpa's over at Sal's place. Our grandpa would make a big deal out of it, and usually made a whole meal with macaroni, maybe some chicken, and a salad. But at home, whatever was in that one pot was what you were eatin'. We'd sit in the kitchen—the dining room was for weekends and holidays—and we'd all be expected to pitch in, takin' this or that outta the freezer to thaw or settin' the table, foldin' the napkins like it was a restaurant. We'd come in from playin' with other kids on the block around 6 or 6:30 p.m., and we'd sit watchin' TV while we ate—*Diff'rent Strokes, Facts of Life, Family Ties.* After that it was homework (our moms were real anal about that) and *Taxi,* then bed, unless it was a Tuesday night—then we were allowed to stay up past 10 p.m. for *Moonlighting.*

ITALIAN MACARONI AND CHEESE

SERVES 4

Red sauce isn't the only thing that's popular in Italian-American houses. Garlic and oil is huge. Our grandmother always used to say she could make anything taste good with garlic and oil. It was handy for when you didn't have time to make a sauce. It was also handy when you needed to get a big pot of macaroni made for dinner—because that's how we ate. It wasn't three, four courses on the table. It was one big pot of somethin'. This was a weeknight staple for us—just simple macaroni with garlic, oil, and some pecorino.

Salt

1 pound linguine

½ cup olive oil

2½ tablespoons chopped garlic

1 teaspoon red pepper flakes

3 tablespoons chopped fresh flat-leaf parsley

2 tablespoons salted butter

1 teaspoon black pepper

10 fresh basil leaves, chopped

½ cup grated pecorino

Bring a large saucepot of salted water to a boil. Add the linguine and cook according to the package directions until al dente. Drain the pasta, reserving ½ cup of the cooking water. Set aside the pasta and reserved cooking water.

In a large frying pan, combine the olive oil, garlic, red pepper flakes, and 1 teaspoon salt. Sauté over medium-high heat until the garlic is golden brown. Add the parsley and remove from the heat.

Add the pasta to the pan with the garlic and oil, then add the reserved pasta water, butter, black pepper, basil, and pecorino and toss to combine and melt the butter and cheese.

SALTING PASTA WATER

All our pasta recipes call for cooking with salted water. It adds more flavor, sure, but really the point of adding salt is to help the water come to a boil more quickly. As for how much salt you should use, 3 to 4 tablespoons will do it.

❀

PEAS AND MACARONI

SERVES 4

This reminds us of coming home from school. It was always, "What're we eatin' tonight?" "Peas and macaroni." It was cheap, it was fast, and it was also very delicious. Healthy, too, probably, with the peas. You start by browning the onions with the meat so they get soft and caramelized, then you add the peas and a coupla scoops of tomato sauce. And while the pasta—usually the little baby shells— is cooking, you chop up a bunch of potatoes and fry 'em. Everybody did this a little different—Fran's mom liked to put the potatoes right in with the grease from the sausage and onions. Sal's mom liked to fry 'em separate in a frying pan. We liked it better that way, because it had an almost French fry effect. But it's all good—especially when you top it with some grated cheese.

Salt

2 pounds ground beef or sweet Italian sausages, casings removed

2 Spanish onions, sliced

4 small potatoes, peeled and cut into cubes

Black pepper

4 cups Marinara Sauce (page 142)

2 (15-ounce) cans green peas, drained

1 pound short pasta, like ditalini

8 tablespoons (1 stick) salted butter

Grated pecorino, for serving

Bring a large pot of salted water to a boil.

In a large pan, brown the sausages over medium-high heat, breaking them up with your spoon as they cook. When some of the fat from the sausages has rendered into the pan, add the onions and cook until they're soft. If you want to try it Fran's mom's way, add the potatoes now, with some salt and pepper to taste, and let the mixture simmer until the potatoes are easily pierced with a knife or fork, 5 to 7 minutes. Otherwise, throw in the marinara and the peas, and let simmer while you make the potatoes in a separate pan. If you're goin' that route, heat some oil in a frying pan and cook the potatoes with some salt and pepper until they're golden on all sides, 5 to 7 minutes.

While the sausages and potatoes cook, cook the pasta in boiling water according to the package directions until al dente. Drain the pasta and add it to the sausage mixture. Stir in the butter until it has melted, toss, and serve with some cheese sprinkled on top.

CAULIFLOWER AND MACARONI

SERVES 4

If we had to pick one person we automatically think of when it comes to this dish, it would be our grandfather—sittin' at the table, usin' paper towels instead of napkins, a big bowl of grated cheese with a spoon in it sittin' nearby, and him just eatin' cauliflower and macaroni. He made this dish at least a few times a week, which is how our mothers started makin' it. It's one of Sal's mom Bella's favorite things to make in the house and was probably one of the top ten things we ate during the week. This dish, along with Cauliflower Fritters (page 65), was a great way to get us to eat our cauliflower.

1 head cauliflower

½ cup olive oil

10 garlic cloves, sliced

1 (16-ounce) can tomato sauce

2 teaspoons salt

½ teaspoon black pepper

1 pound of your favorite pasta
  (Grandpa liked linguine)

6 tablespoons grated pecorino

Peel the green leaves from the outside of the cauliflower, trim off the stem, and give the head a rinse under cold water, pat it dry, then give it a rough chop.

In a medium saucepan, heat the olive oil, garlic, and cauliflower over medium heat until hot. When the garlic begins to brown, add the tomato sauce, salt, pepper, and 1 cup water and bring to a simmer. Cook until the cauliflower is fork-tender but not completely mushy, 15 to 20 minutes.

Bring a pot of salted water to a boil. Cook the pasta according to the package directions until al dente. Drain the pasta and toss it in the pan with the cauliflower mixture. Sprinkle with the cheese and serve.

BEANS AND MACARONI

SERVES 10

In the restaurant, we'd call this dish pasta e fagioli *("pasta fajool"), and we were known for it in Staten Island. But it's really just a fancy way of sayin' pasta and beans. This was another dish that our mothers loved to make in the house, or if we were at our grandparents' house, it would be the pasta course.*

At the restaurant, this was more of a soup. You'd have the beans and broth in a pot, ready to be portioned out, and when you needed an order you'd pour a coupla ladles over macaroni that was already made, 'cause if you cooked the macaroni in the pot, it'd turn to mush. At home, though, you cook the macaroni right into the soup mix. First, you take your bacon, veg, and tomato sauce and cook, cook, cook. Then come the beans and the stock, then the macaroni, right inta the pot. That way, the starch from the pasta thickens the whole thing, almost like a gumbo. A lot of people use prosciutto, or at least they don't use Oscar Mayer bacon. But we can tell. Seriously—if you don't use Oscar Mayer bacon, it's not really our recipe.

1 cup olive oil

2 pounds bacon, preferably
  Oscar Mayer, chopped

2 white onions, chopped

1½ bunches celery, chopped

2 tablespoons chopped garlic

1 bunch fresh flat-leaf parsley, leaves
  and stems chopped

3 cups Cooked Sauce (page 141)

8 (14-ounce) cans cannellini beans
  (do not drain)

2 quarts chicken broth

8 pinches (1½ to 2 teaspoons) of salt

1 tablespoon black pepper

2 pounds ditalini pasta

Grated pecorino, for serving

In a large saucepot, heat the olive oil over medium heat. Add the bacon and cook until it is crispy, about 10 minutes.

Add the onions, celery, garlic, and parsley and sauté until the onions are soft, about 5 minutes. Stir in the tomato sauce and cook for 10 minutes more.

Empty the beans into the pot, then pour the stock into the empty cans to make sure you've cleaned out every last bit (that's what's going to thicken the sauce, so make sure you don't skip this step), then pour the broth into the soup. Season with the salt and pepper and bring the sauce to a boil. Add the pasta and cook according to the package directions until al dente. Serve with pecorino for sprinkling.

VARIATION: ADD SOME ESCAROLE

If you want to get some greens into this, take 3 heads of escarole and rinse 'em really well in cold water to get out all the grit. Give 'em a rough chop and add 'em to the pot with the beans.

ESCAROLE JUICE

Whenever our grandmother made plain boiled escarole, she'd save the green juice that was left over and drink it. She believed it was healthy for you, good for the stomach and digestion. Then she'd put the leftover green juice in the fridge and every once in a while warm it up and have a glass.

CHICHI BEANS AND RICE

SERVES 2 TO 4

This was another thing that was on the table at least once a week. We were the only people we knew who had white rice with tomato sauce on it, but it was delicious, not to mention cheap, filling, and easy to make. You just had to take the sauce, heat it up, throw a can of chichi beans in it (spelled ceci *but pronounced "chichi"—either way, they're chickpeas), pour it over rice and throw some grated cheese over it, and that was it. That's what you were eatin'.*

2 tablespoons olive oil

4 garlic cloves, minced

1 (28-ounce) can chichi beans, drained and rinsed

Salt and black pepper

2 cups Cooked Sauce (page 141)

1 cup dry white rice, cooked according
    to the package directions

In a saucepan, heat the olive oil over medium heat. Add the garlic and sauté until it begins to brown. Add the beans and season with salt and pepper. After 2 to 3 minutes, pour in the tomato sauce and ½ cup water. Bring to a boil, then reduce the heat to maintain a simmer and cook for about 10 minutes. Mix in the cooked rice and serve.

FRANKS AND BEANS

SERVES 4

This definitely wasn't Italian, but it was delicious and it was fast. Fran's mom would make this for us by puttin' some baked beans down in a pan, then the hot dogs sliced longways, and then some Oscar Mayer bacon (it had to be Oscar Mayer), and she topped it all with maple syrup. It would go in the oven just like that. We have no idea where it came from or who invented it, but we're just happy they did.

3 (8-ounce) cans baked beans with pork

8 hot dogs, preferably Sabrett, halved lengthwise

½ cup maple syrup

Preheat the oven to 350°F.

Pour the beans into a casserole dish, then layer the hot dog slices on top. Drizzle with the syrup and bake for 20 minutes, or until the hot dogs start to get crispy.

Fran, Fran's mom, and Fran's friend Karl

SWISS CHARD GUMBO WITH BACON AND RICE

SERVED 1 TO 6

Swiss chard has a really delicious, unique flavor compared to a lot of other greens. And it was something our grandma really liked to cook. This dish wasn't as popular in our house as, say, beans and macaroni, but it was very tasty, and we knew how much our grandmother loved it. We love makin' this now because it brings back a lotta memories.

The greens get cooked up in rendered bacon grease—we're big believers in Oscar Mayer here—then cooked down with just a little salt and pepper, and whatever ends of cheese you have lyin' around. Maybe a couple pieces of provolone or pecorino. Then when the rice gets added at the end, it gets all thick, like a stew or a gumbo. It's delicious on its own and definitely delicious piled on top of some Italian bread.

½ cup olive oil

6 ounces (6 slices) Oscar Mayer bacon, cut into ⅛-inch pieces

12 garlic cloves, halved

3 bunches Swiss chard, rinsed, stems stripped and leaves cut into 2-inch strips

8 cups chicken stock

1 cup Marinara Sauce (page 142)

4 teaspoons black pepper

3 cups long-grain white rice, like Carolina

1 cup grated pecorino

In a medium saucepot, heat the olive oil over medium heat. Add the bacon and cook until it's crispy. Add the garlic and cook until it's just beginning to brown. Add about two-thirds of the Swiss chard, the chicken stock, marinara, and pepper and bring to a boil. Add the rice, then reduce the heat to low, cover, and simmer until the rice is cooked through and most of the liquid has been absorbed, about 20 minutes. Remove from the heat, stir in the remaining chard and the cheese, and serve.

LENTIL SOUP WITH A HAM BONE

SERVES 8

In the restaurant we had a joke—anytime someone would say, "Got any specials tonight?" we'd say, "Yeah, stuffed lentils." Sometimes they were all confused and said, "What are they stuffed with?" Got us every time.

This is a dish that our grandmother cooked a lot, so it made sense that our mothers cooked it too. Even though we didn't call a lot of things by their proper Italian names, this dish got that distinction: pasta e lenticchie—*probably because it was Frank Sinatra's favorite dish. But it's okay by us if you just call it lentil soup.*

3 tablespoons olive oil

1 large onion, chopped

3 garlic cloves, minced

4½ cups chicken broth

2 ham hocks

1 (12-ounce) can tomato paste

1 (28-ounce) can crushed tomatoes

2 medium carrots, diced

2 small green frying peppers or
    cubanelles, seeded and finely chopped

2 cups dried lentils, rinsed

½ teaspoon salt

1 teaspoon black pepper

1 pound acini di pepe or pastina

Grated Parmigiano-Reggiano, for serving

In a large saucepot, heat the oil over medium-high heat. Add the onion and sauté until tender, about 3 minutes. Add the garlic and cook for 1 minute more.

Pour 2 cups water into the pot, along with the chicken broth, ham hocks, tomato paste, tomatoes, carrots, green peppers, lentils, salt, and black pepper. Bring the soup to a boil, then reduce the heat to low, cover, and simmer for 10 minutes, or until the lentils are tender.

In a separate large pot, bring 8 cups water to a boil, add the pasta, and cook according to the package directions until al dente. Drain the pasta and mix it into the soup. Top with grated cheese and serve.

PASTINA WITH GRATED CHEESE

SERVES 4

If we were ever home sick from school, this is what our mothers would make for us. We don't know what kind of magical healing properties it had, but it was like medicine.

Pastina is a type of pasta that's shaped like teeny tiny stars. They're almost microscopic they're so small, like the size of ants. You cook it in salted water and finish it with butter, grated cheese, a little bit of salt, and that's it. We're feelin' good just thinkin' about it.

Salt

1 (12-ounce) box pastina pasta

8 tablespoons (1 stick) salted butter

½ cup grated pecorino

In a large saucepot, bring 16 cups salted water to a boil. Add the pasta and cook, stirring frequently, for 5 to 7 minutes, or until al dente. Drain the pasta in a fine-mesh strainer (the pastina will slip through the holes of a colander), then scoop the pasta into pasta bowls. Top each portion with 2 tablespoons of the butter and some grated cheese.

VARIATION:

If you were sick on a weekday, you got pastina or white rice, but if it was a Sunday, you would get some raviolis with butter instead of sauce.

FRIED SPAGHETTI PIE

SERVES 1

Whenever we'd cook spaghetti in the house, what we'd do is put a couple of ladles of sauce into the pot so it wouldn't all stick together. Then we'd put it on a plate and scoop another ladle of sauce over the top. Then whatever you didn't finish, you'd put in the fridge. And when it got cold, something magical happened. That spaghetti coated in sauce got real starchy, so when you fried it, it stuck together like a big pancake. All you gotta do is add egg—not enough to make it a spaghetti omelet, but just enough to keep everything together like glue and also give the pancake a nice golden crust. After that, just throw in some grated cheese, and if you have some parsley, throw some chopped parsley in there. Then fry it up until it's almost burnt, like crispy Cantonese noodles, get some grated cheese on it, and slice it like a pie. Delicious.

2 large eggs

½ pound leftover spaghetti with Cooked Sauce (page 141)
or Marinara Sauce (page 142)

½ cup grated pecorino, plus more for serving

½ cup olive oil

In a large bowl, beat the eggs. Add the spaghetti and the cheese and mix well.

Heat the olive oil in a large nonstick frying pan over medium to high heat until it's sizzling hot (you can test it by carefully adding a tiny drop of water to the pan—it should evaporate on contact).

Scoop the pasta into the pan and shape it into a flat pancake. Cook until the bottom is deeply golden, then flip it over. Don't worry if it's not the perfect pancake flip. Cook until the other side is golden. Top with more grated cheese, slice like a pizza, and eat.

BAKED ZITI WITH RICOTTA

SERVES 4 TO 6

If you didn't have time to make lasagna, you made baked ziti. But it wasn't just convenient; it was insanely delicious too—especially because of how we did the ricotta. In our house, ricotta was like a condiment. The way some people have ketchup, we had ricotta. On Sunday, when we had macaroni, there was always ricotta on the table. You'd take a scoop and you'd throw it on your pasta cold. Now, most people, when they're makin' baked ziti, they'll put down the sauce and then mix the ricotta right into it. We don't—we leave it in a bunch of big dollops, like the way you put sour cream on a potato. That way, with every bite you get a little sauce, a little pasta, and a little cheese. And because good ricotta doesn't melt or get really hot, there's a nice contrast between the warm ziti and the cool ricotta.

1 pound ziti

7 cups Cooked Sauce (page 141)

2 cups ricotta cheese

1 cup grated pecorino

½ bunch fresh flat-leaf parsley, leaves and stems chopped

2 pounds Polly-O mozzarella, sliced

Preheat the oven to 450°F.

Bring a large pot of water to a boil. Cook the ziti according to the package directions until al dente. Drain well and set aside.

Coat the bottom of a large casserole dish with a layer of the sauce. Top with a layer of the pasta, a layer of ricotta (generously dolloped on using a tablespoon), some of the pecorino, some of the parsley, then the mozzarella. Continue layering until there's no more pasta remaining.

Spread one last layer of mozzarella over the top, then one last layer of tomato sauce, and then top it all off with the leftover pecorino and a sprinkle of parsley. Bake for 20 to 25 minutes, or until the cheese has browned.

"SPITZ"

SERVES 2 TO 3

This dish was a big favorite when we weren't eating peas or beans and macaroni. My grand-mother called it spitz, short for "spitzedad." She'd sauté the garlic and oil and chicken wings all at the same time until everything got nice and brown and the chicken had given up as much fat as possible. Then she'd throw in a couple of cups of starchy water from the macaroni—in this case, spaghetti or linguine—or chicken stock and let the meat cook to the point where you just looked at it and it fell off the bone. She'd put all the pasta in a bowl, pour the whole fryin' pan with all the grease and garlic and oil right over it, add some grated cheese, and that was it. It was delicious.

We were in the Dominican Republic in Santo Domingo a few months ago with a buddy who has family out there. There was this kid on the side of the road sellin' chicharones. He had a big BBQ made out of a fifty-gallon drum and this contraption made out of a propane tank and was fryin' 'em up right in the street. He sold 'em by the pound and would ask, "You want sauce on it?" That sauce was so friggin' good—one of the best sauces we ever had. You would eat it off the floor it was so good. We asked him what was in it and he said orange juice and Sazón—you know, those Spanish seasonings—and chicken grease. Our point is, chicken grease is good. And so is this dish.

½ cup olive oil

6 chicken wings (not Buffalo wings, actual chicken wings)

2 tablespoons chopped garlic

1 teaspoon salt

1 teaspoon black pepper

½ teaspoon red pepper flakes

2 tablespoons chopped fresh flat-leaf parsley

3 cups chicken broth

½ pound spaghetti or linguine

In a deep frying pan or medium saucepot, heat the oil over medium-high heat. Add the chicken and brown it on both sides, adding the garlic when you flip the chicken to cook the second side. Add the salt, black pepper, red pepper flakes, and parsley and deglaze the pan with the chicken broth, scraping up all the good brown bits from the bottom of the pan. Let the mixture simmer for 30 minutes, until the chicken meat is falling off the bones.

Bring a large pot of salted water to a boil. Cook the pasta according to the package directions until al dente. Drain the pasta and add it to the pot with the chicken, toss, and serve.

CHICKEN AND LARD

SERVES 4 TO 6

Fran's grandmother—or step-grandmother, really—was Aunt Tina. Fran's grandfather Francis, who was Portuguese, married her after he divorced his first wife, a Sicilian woman, which was pretty much unheard of back then. He ended up marrying Tina, a Portuguese woman twenty-odd years younger than him. Well, Aunt Tina was one of the best cooks that anybody knew. Even Fran's mom, Joy, loved her cookin'—especially because it was so different from all the Italian food she grew up eating—and chicken and lard was one of her favorite dishes. She loved eatin' the tender meat from the underside of the chicken, and she really loved the wings. It used to make Aunt Tina so mad because Grandpa Francis—or "Chico," as she called him— also liked the wings, so she ended up having to buy extra wings for when we were comin' over.

Aunt Tina ended up teaching Joy how to make this dish and told her the three secrets: You gotta use lard; you gotta cook the chicken low and slow; and you gotta use a can of warm beer.

3 large white onions, cut into wedges

4 russet potatoes, peeled and
    cut lengthwise into wedges

4 sweet potatoes, peeled and
    cut lengthwise into wedges

¼ pound lard (look in the dairy aisle,
    near the butter)

4 chicken breasts

4 chicken legs

4 chicken thighs

4 chicken wings

1 cup olive oil

½ cup salt

½ cup black pepper

½ cup granulated garlic

½ can Budweiser beer, warm

2 tablespoons chopped fresh Italian parsley

Preheat the oven to 300°F.

In a roasting pan, make a layer of onions and potatoes. Add the lard.

Coat the chicken pieces in the olive oil, then season them generously with the salt, pepper, and garlic. Put the chicken in the roasting pan on top of the vegetables and lard.

Cover the pan with foil and bake for 2½ hours. Raise the oven temperature to 350°F, remove the foil, add the beer, and cook for 1½ hours, uncovered, so the chicken skin gets crispy and the juices and beer reduce. Sprinkle with parsley and serve.

PORK CUTLETS WITH VINEGAR PEPPERS

SERVES 6

If there was a special on pork chops, this is what was for dinner. Although pork chops are pretty cheap anyway (and if you have to feed a bunch of hungry kids, it's a whole lot cheaper than steak). All our moms needed to do was fry 'em up and make a quick sauce with the peppers, which we always had in the pantry because they last forever and have great flavor. Sometimes they'd serve 'em more American-style, with applesauce or duck sauce, but this was by far the best.

4 large eggs

1 cup whole milk

½ cup Dry Bread Crumbs (page 79)

6 (1-inch-thick) boneless pork chops, butterflied (ask your butcher to do this)

2 cups plus 3 tablespoons olive oil

4 garlic cloves, chopped

1 cup pickled pepper brine

1 cup marsala wine

4 teaspoons all-purpose flour

2 teaspoons butter

3 pinches of salt

1 pinch of black pepper

1 pinch of red pepper flakes

½ cup hot peperoncini peppers

In a large baking dish or bowl, beat together the eggs and milk. Fill another large bowl with the bread crumbs.

Submerge each pork cutlet in the egg mixture, then immediately transfer to the bread crumbs. Make sure the chops are completely coated with the crumbs.

In large frying pan, heat 2 cups of the olive oil over low heat until shimmering. Fry the pork chops in the hot oil until golden brown, 5 to 6 minutes. If you can't fit all the cutlets in the pan at once, fry them in batches. Transfer the finished cutlets to a paper towel to cool.

In a medium saucepan, heat the remaining 3 tablespoons of olive oil over medium heat. Add the garlic and cook until brown. Add the brine and marsala and cook, stirring rapidly, for 5 minutes. Add the flour, butter, salt, black pepper, and red pepper flakes and continue stirring until the sauce has thickened, about 2 minutes. Add in the peperoncini peppers.

Pour the sauce over the cutlets and serve.

ITALIAN ROAST BEEF OVER WONDER BREAD

SERVES 6

This is something our grandmother made a lot, and it was pretty basic roast beef. Except for one thing: She used our grandfather's drill to make holes so she could stuff it. She'd make them about the size of a dime and then use her fingers to shove in some garlic, parsley, and grated cheese. We guess you could just use a knife, but it doesn't seem like nearly as much fun. Fran's mom would sometimes use an electric knife to do it, but we wouldn't recommend it—it makes the meat taste like a hairdryer or something.

You can serve the roast beef on its own, or you can do it like Grandma did and pile slices on Wonder Bread and top the whole thing with gravy.

4 pounds top round beef

6 tablespoons chopped garlic

1 bunch fresh flat-leaf parsley, leaves and stems chopped

6 tablespoons grated pecorino

½ cup olive oil

Salt and black pepper

2 white onions, sliced

4 beef bouillon cubes

1 tablespoon all-purpose flour

1 tablespoon salted butter

Preheat the oven to 375°F.

With a power drill, carve a dime-size hole in the center of the beef all the way through the meat. If using a knife, insert the knife so it goes all the way through the meat, then do it again with the knife at a 90-degree angle to the first cut, so that the two slices make an X. Stuff the garlic, parsley, and cheese into the meat from both sides. Liberally coat the outside of the beef with olive oil and season with salt and pepper.

Spread the onions to cover the bottom of a medium baking pan. Place the beef on top and bake for 30 minutes. Reduce the oven temperature to 250°F and bake for 15 minutes more. Once the inside temperature of the beef registers 135°F on a meat thermometer, it's ready.

While the roast beef is cooking, make the gravy. In a medium saucepot, bring 3 cups of water to a boil. Stir in the bouillon cubes, stirring until the bouillon has completely dissolved. Add the flour and butter to the pot and whisk until smooth. Cook until the

mixture has reduced to a thick, gravy-like consistency, 2 to 3 minutes. Pull it off the heat and serve over the roast beef with the onions from the bottom of the pan.

Grandma Connie at Bella's on Clinton Street, Brooklyn

DEPRESSION MEATBALLS

MAKES ABOUT 10 MEATBALLS

Back when times were tough, most people used bread crumbs to stretch their meat, whether it was for meatballs or meat loaf. You could stretch 2 pounds of meat into 4 pounds of food that way. But when things were really bad, and there was no meat at all, you had to improvise. Especially during the Depression days, our grandmother had to figure out how to cook with nothing. She'd make these "meatballs," which were just bread crumbs, parsley, cheese, and garlic, and then fry 'em like little matzo balls or croquettes. Growin' up, luckily, our moms made these just because they're delicious. If they were already breading chicken or pork cutlets or shrimp Milanese, they'd take the leftover crumbs, throw a couple eggs in there, and cook 'em up.

4 large eggs

3 cups Secret Bread Crumbs (page 82)

1 cup grated pecorino

4 garlic cloves, minced

3 tablespoons chopped fresh flat-leaf parsley

¼ cup olive oil

In a medium bowl, combine the eggs, bread crumbs, cheese, garlic, and parsley and mix well. Use your hands to make golf ball–size balls, then flatten them.

Heat the oil in a skillet over medium heat and fry the meatballs until golden on all sides. Transfer to a paper towel and enjoy.

FRANKIE'S VEAL CUTLETS

SERVES 4

As you've probably noticed, our food always comes with a story, and this dish is no different. This one starts with Fran's father's father—the original Francis Garcia. He was Portuguese, which is how the name "Garcia" got into our Italian family. Our grandmother was the only one of her twelve sisters to marry a non-Italian. But no one cared because Francis was a successful immigration lawyer. He was the first Portuguese lawyer admitted to the bar and he went on to pass an amendment to the Bill of Rights. The guy even went to three presidential inaugurations. And even better, he was a Staten Islander.

Fran's dad, Francis Garcia II, didn't exactly follow in his father's footsteps—he and Fran's mom had seven or eight businesses that failed before he took a city job with the transit authority. And his favorite thing to eat was this dish, which his mother made for him.

When Fran left his mom's restaurant at twenty-three, he opened his own shop, Ciao Bella, on Main Street in Staten Island. He only ran it for a year—he sold it to some Albanians for a decent profit after turnin' around the business—but people still talk about the place. Just the other day someone was at our Fourteenth Street location askin' about it. And the cops all remember it since there was a police station just down the street. Well, this was somethin' that Fran always made for his dad, just the way he liked it—a fried cutlet topped with tomato and onion, drizzled with olive oil, and seasoned with nothin' but salt, pepper, and oregano.

2 large eggs

½ cup whole milk

1 cup Dry Bread Crumbs (page 79)

4 (4-ounce) veal cutlets, pounded thin
   (to about ⅛ inch)

¾ cup olive oil

1 large tomato, sliced into
   ¼-inch wheels

½ medium white onion, sliced

2 pinches of salt

2 pinches of pepper

2 pinches of oregano

In a medium bowl, whisk together the eggs and milk until well combined.

In a second medium bowl, add the bread crumbs.

Place the cutlets in the egg and milk mixture and let them soak, completely submerged, for a minute. Transfer them to the bread crumbs and generously bread them to coat.

Put a medium frying pan over medium heat and add ½ cup of olive oil. When the oil shimmers, add the cutlets and fry until golden brown on both sides, 1 to 2 minutes a side.

Remove the cutlets and top with a layer of tomato slices and a layer of onion slices. Pour the remaining olive oil over the top, then sprinkle with the salt, pepper, and oregano.

Fran with his dad

VEAL AND MUSHROOM STEW
SERVES 4 TO 6

Frank Roma was a Staten Island legend. No joke. In the seventies, eighties, and even the nineties, his restaurant, Roma's, was an institution, and we're willin' to bet that if you were livin' there then, you'll know exactly who this guy was. Well, in 1995 he had to close his restaurant. Thing was, the guy was like ninety-two, ninety-three years old. Most people would retire, right? Not Frank Roma. He had that old-school workin' mentality—he needed to work. And the guy could still freakin' cook. So he came to Fran's mother at Basille's and asked her for a job. At first she was like, "Frank, I can't afford you," but ultimately she paid him basically to just have him around, give him a place to hang his hat and cook. It wasn't really like he could keep up; it was like havin' your grandfather in the kitchen. He'd come in when he felt like it, prep a few specials, and then be sittin' in the back on a bucket with a towel on his head. But the best thing he did was he taught us things. He was always tellin' us how we could save here and there just by using ingredients more than one way, usin' scraps—"Don't waste nothin'," he used to say. Some of the things we politely ignored, like using margarine instead of butter—he was always tellin' us it was cheaper but still had butter flavor, but we didn't like how it separated in the sauce and got all nasty—but one thing we really ran with was this stew. He'd make it using all the veal scraps that you couldn't butcher into cutlets. Then he'd cook it slow with sherry wine and mushrooms, and it was just outta this world.

1 cup all-purpose flour

2 pounds veal, cubed

4 tablespoons (½ stick) butter

¼ cup olive oil

2 (8-ounce) packages of button mushrooms, sliced into thirds

2 white onions, finely chopped

½ bunch fresh flat-leaf parsley, leaves and stems chopped

2 cups sherry cooking wine

2 cups beef stock

1 (6-ounce) can tomato paste

4 pinches of black pepper

2 dried bay leaves

Put the flour in a medium bowl. Dredge the veal in the flour so it's generously coated.

In a large saucepan, heat the butter and olive oil over medium heat. Add the veal cubes and sear the meat until golden brown on all sides.

Add the mushrooms and onions and cook until the onions soften and the mushrooms get tender, about 10 minutes.

Throw in the parsley, then stir in the sherry, beef stock, tomato paste, and pepper and cook for 5 to 7 minutes before adding the bay leaves.

Bring the pot to a simmer and cook for 1½ hours, stirring occasionally. Every now and then stop what you're doin' and smell the stew. Isn't that nice? Makes us feel like dancin'.

STUFFED MEAT LOAF

SERVES 4

It doesn't get much better than meat loaf stuffed with Genoa salami, ham, hard-boiled eggs, and provolone and topped with bacon. This wasn't something that showed up on our table, but the recipe comes from a friend's ninety-year-old aunt, Louisa Marielli, who's Staten Island through and through.

2 pounds ground beef

5 large eggs

1 cup Secret Bread Crumbs (page 82)

1 bunch fresh flat-leaf parsley, leaves and stems chopped

½ cup grated pecorino

2 pinches of black pepper

4 hard-boiled eggs, sliced

¼ pound thinly sliced Genoa salami

¼ pound thinly sliced boiled ham

¼ pound thinly sliced provolone

5 russet potatoes, cut into wedges

1 onion, sliced

1 (15-ounce) can green peas

2 (15-ounce) cans tomato sauce, preferably Del Monte

6 slices bacon

Preheat the oven to 375°F.

In a large bowl, mix together the ground beef, raw eggs, bread crumbs, parsley, cheese, and pepper like you're makin' meatballs.

Spread the mixture evenly in a large baking pan. Layer the hard-boiled eggs, salami, ham, and cheese on top. Then, starting on one of the shorter ends, carefully "roll" the meat closed so it forms a loaf. Add the potatoes, onion, and peas to the pan around the meat loaf, then pour in the tomato sauce. Fill the two tomato sauce cans with water and add that too. Lay the bacon over the meatloaf and transfer to the oven. Bake for 1¼ hours, or until the potatoes are soft.

UNCLE VITO'S RABBITS

STEWED, ROASTED, OR COOKED IN SAUCE

Sal's father used to raise rabbits. He'd mate them, look after them for three, four months, then kill 'em and cook 'em. We would play with them and name them, and then, yeah, we'd eat them. Sometimes he'd make us kill 'em too—said it would make us tough. One of his favorite things to do was serve the rabbits to people and tell them it was chicken. Some surprise, huh? Our uncle Frankie would call him a "born-again Barbarian."

But really, they were pretty good. You could make 'em any way you would make chicken too—browned and stewed, roasted in the oven, or cooked in sauce like pizzaiola. All that variation was a good thing because when it was time to kill the rabbits, that meant Sal's family would be eatin' 'em every night for like two weeks straight.

STEWED

SERVES 3

4 tablespoons olive oil

1 (3-pound) rabbit, cut into 2-inch pieces (ask your butcher to do it for you if you're feeling squeamish), washed and patted dry

Salt and black pepper

2 cups all-purpose flour

½ cup dry red wine

1 large Spanish onion, diced

1 bunch carrots, chopped into 1-inch pieces

2 stalks celery, chopped

4 garlic cloves, minced

2 tablespoons tomato paste

4 cups chicken stock

2 sprigs fresh rosemary, tied into a bundle with kitchen twine

4 medium russet potatoes, peeled and quartered

1 (16-ounce) bag frozen peas

1 tablespoon chopped fresh flat-leaf parsley

Preheat the oven to 350°F.

In a large pan, heat 2 to 3 tablespoons of the olive oil over medium-high heat. Season the rabbit with salt and pepper and dredge it in flour until well coated. Add the rabbit to the pan and cook until golden brown and crispy, 10 to 15 minutes. Transfer the pieces to a plate and set aside.

CONTINUED

Add the wine to the pot and let it reduce for about 2 minutes as you scrape the bottom of the pot to loosen any of the good browned bits. Pour the contents of the pan into a cup or small bowl and set aside.

In a large saucepot or Dutch oven, heat the remaining olive oil over medium heat. Add the onion, carrots, celery, and garlic and cook until soft and browned, 10 to 15 minutes. Add the rabbit and the tomato paste and stir just to blend everything together. Pour in the chicken stock and the reserved reduced pan liquid and add the rosemary, then partially cover with a lid and cook for about 30 minutes.

Add the potatoes to the pot, then cover the pot completely with the lid and transfer to the oven. Bake for 1 to 1½ hours, or until the rabbit is fork-tender. Stir in the peas and parsley. Allow the stew to rest, covered, for 15 minutes, then serve.

ROASTED

SERVES 3

1 (3-pound) rabbit, cut into 8 to 10 pieces (ask your butcher to do it for you if you're feeling squeamish), washed and patted dry

1 cup olive oil

2 large onions, sliced

2½ pounds russet potatoes, peeled and cut into cubes

2 sprigs fresh rosemary

3 large red bell peppers, seeded and sliced

3 large yellow bell peppers, seeded and sliced

Salt and black pepper

½ cup beef stock

Preheat the oven to 400°F.

Put the rabbit in a large roasting pan with all the ingredients except the salt, pepper, and stock. Mix, season with salt and pepper, then roast for about 30 minutes. Take the pan out of the oven and turn the rabbit pieces so they brown on both sides. Add the stock and cook for 30 to 40 minutes more, until all the rabbit pieces are golden brown.

COOKED IN SAUCE

SERVES 3

¼ cup olive oil

2 medium white onions, diced

1 (3-pound) rabbit, cut into 1½-inch cubes (ask your butcher to do it for you if you're feeling squeamish), washed and patted dry

6 garlic cloves

4 (24-ounce) jars peeled Italian tomatoes, strained and seeded

Salt and black pepper

1 bunch fresh basil

1 box of your favorite pasta

In a large saucepot, heat the olive oil over medium to high heat. Add the onions and rabbit and brown together. When lightly browned, stir in the garlic with a spoon. When everything is a nice golden brown, add the tomatoes and season with salt and pepper. Bring the mixture to a boil, then lower the heat to medium.

Cook, uncovered, for 1½ hours, stirring occasionally with a wooden spoon to prevent the sauce from sticking to the bottom of the pan.

Remove the pot from the heat, add the basil, and let it sit for 30 minutes more.

Meanwhile, bring a pot of salted water to a boil. Cook your favorite pasta. Serve the rabbit spooned over the top of the pasta. The kids will think it's chicken!

Top: Sal, Grandpa Dominick, and Sal's mother, Bella

9

LENT FRIDAYS, SUNNY SUMMER DAYS,

· FROM THE OCEAN ·

AND GRANDPA DOMINICK'S LEGACY

We ate a lotta seafood in our house, and not just because of Lent. Actually, the only reason we ever knew it was Friday during Lent was because we were always ridiculously busy at the restaurant. We're not talkin' about a little bit more business—we're talkin' if you sold $2,000 worth of pizza on a normal night, you were at least doubling that on Fridays. It was all Italians and Irish Catholics in the neighborhood, so we'd be madhouse crazy. And all the orders would be for eggplant pies, seafood pies—no meat. I guess we shoulda known it was Lent because of church, but it was what it was.

Lent or not, when we were eatin' seafood it was because the love for it ran in our family. Our great-grandpa Gregory Auditorre, who owned a pastry shop, he was always cookin' fish in the store. Seriously—you'd walk in expecting to smell cookies and all you could smell was garlic and oil. But the poor guy, his wife didn't cook. She kept the house spotless, but she couldn't make a thing. So our great-grandfather, he did all the cookin'. And since he had to be downstairs runnin' the pastry business, he'd cook for the two of them then bring it upstairs for lunch and dinner. He'd always be makin' those heavy fishes like bluefish with garlic and parsley. It would smell delicious, but that's all you could smell when you walked in. Sal's mom, Bella, remembers sayin' something to him about it once. All he said was, "What do you want me to do? I gotta eat!"

But our grandpa Dominick was the big fish guy in the family. He came to America when he was sixteen, but the time he did spend in Sicily, he spent in a fishing village. So he was always around the water and fishing culture. He loved fishin'—that was his thing. In the summertime we'd go down to the marina and hang out on his boat, then watch him make Crab Sauce (page 184) on the piers. And whenever we'd go over to his house, he was always makin' some kinda seafood—whiting, or "Whities," as he called 'em, with Lemon and Onion (page 196) or Mussels Marinara with Linguine (page 188) or a big pot of Seafood Fra Diavolo Sauce (page 143).

Most of these recipes are perfect for when the weather gets warm. For us, that always meant havin' dinner in the backyard. In Staten Island, *everybody* had the same yard. It was exactly like what you saw in *Easy Money*—the cookie-cutter thirty-foot by fifty-foot lot, a chain-link fence with green slats runnin' through it, an aboveground pool, a little bit of grass, a little deck, and a grill. In the summertime, everybody would be out there, so you could see what your neighbors had goin' on. You knew you were cookin' something good when other people started showin' up at your door with a plate.

....

HOLY MACKEREL

SERVES 2

Our grandfather loved makin' this dish and would actually call it Holy Mackerel too. He'd buy whole mackerels, flour 'em, and fry 'em with the skin on. The flour acted like a kind of roux and would thicken up the sauce a bit, which was basically just oil and garlic, white wine, and a splash of red sauce.

1 cup all-purpose flour

2 teaspoons salt, plus more as needed

1 teaspoon black pepper, plus more as needed

2 medium mackerels, gutted, cleaned, and butterflied

1 cup olive oil

1 tablespoon salted butter

1 large Spanish onion, halved and cut into 1-inch slices

½ cup white wine

¾ cup (or 1 [6-ounce] ladle) Marinara Sauce (page 142)

½ cup chopped fresh flat-leaf parsley

1 lemon, cut into wedges, for serving

In a large bowl, combine the flour, salt, and pepper. Toss the mackerel in the flour and dredge inside and out. Shake off any excess flour and lay the mackerel on a plate.

In a frying pan, heat the olive oil over medium-high heat until it shimmers. Line a plate with paper towels. Fry the mackerel in the hot oil until golden brown, then transfer to the paper towel–lined plate and set aside.

Drain half the oil out of the pan, then add the butter, onion, and salt and pepper to taste and cook until the onions are soft but not caramelized. When just about there, pour in the wine and scrape up all the good stuff from the bottom of the pan. Let the wine cook out until the pan is almost dry but not quite, then add the red sauce and toss in the parsley. Smother the mackerel with the onions and serve with wedges of lemon.

SANDSHARK

WITH RED WINE, BUDWEISER, ONIONS, AND POTATOES

SERVES 2

Because our grandfather grew up in Sicily, he was always eatin' seafood—whiting, baccalà, sardines, crabs, mussels, clams, lobsters. After he passed, we would still go fishing all the time. One day we weren't catching anything; we just kept getting the same friggin' sandshark. Nobody ever kept a sandshark—they'd get mad at it and throw it back in. They called it "dog fish." But we said "Screw it, we'll keep it and eat it." So we took it back to Fran's mother's house to cook it. We were with our friend Eddy, who is an expert fisherman, and he skinned this thing, no problem. And it's not that easy. But this kid was such a pro that he just peeled off the skin. It was late, so instead of making a soup and stinkin' up Fran's mother's house, we decided to throw it on the BBQ. We took a big roasting pan, cut up some potatoes and onions, threw in some butter, dried parsley, salt, and pepper, and then laid the fish down. Normally we'd add some white wine 'cause we were makin' fish, but all we had was this bottle of Merlot from some vineyard in Jersey and a can of Budweiser.

When we tell you that this was the most delicious thing we ever cooked by accident, we're not jokin'. Now every time we go fishing we keep the sandsharks and cook 'em like this and then we all fight over the burnt bits soaked with all that delicious grease from the fish. You could do this with bluefish too. Just make sure you scrape up all the good stuff from the bottom of the pan. You'll get more of it if you cook this over direct heat on a grill, but you can make it in the oven too.

1 large sandshark or bluefish,
  cleaned and skinned

3 large Spanish onions, sliced

8 russet potatoes, cut into cubes

8 tablespoons (1 stick) salted butter

3 tablespoons lard

2 cups red wine, like Merlot

3 tablespoons dried parsley

2 teaspoons black pepper

2 teaspoons salt

1 tablespoon garlic powder

1 bay leaf

2 teaspoons fresh thyme

1 (12-ounce) can Budweiser

Heat a grill to medium heat or preheat the oven to 400°F.

In a large roasting pan, combine all of the ingredients except for the beer. Cover with foil and place on the grill and close the lid, or place the pan in the oven. Cook for 1½ hours, then remove the foil. Continue cooking, checking every now and then until most of the liquid has evaporated. Add the can of beer. Keep cooking until the beer has evaporated.

With a metal spatula, serve up the fish along with the scrapings from the bottom of the pan.

GRANDPA DOMINICK'S ICED TEA

MAKES 4 CUPS

Our grandfather used to love makin' iced tea. He thought he had a secret recipe, which basically meant just adding triple the amount of 4C iced tea mix than called for on the box, plus about a cup of table sugar. He'd just keep throwin' it in. It was the sweetest tea you ever tasted in your entire life, so sweet it could rot your teeth and thick enough that you could put a knife in it and it would stand up straight. You could use it for pancake batter. He'd serve it with crushed ice and eat it with a spoon. Then whatever he didn't drink right away, he'd go the extra mile and store it in glass Tropicana bottles so It got even colder in the fridge.

1 package iced tea mix

1 cup sugar

Juice of 2 lemons

Make the iced tea according to the package instructions, doubling the amount of mix called for. Stir in the sugar and lemon juice and serve over crushed ice.

CRAB SAUCE

SERVES 4

In the summertime, our parents would take us down to the dock two, three days a week. My grandfather had a big boat at the marina where he'd be almost every day—like the mayor of the place. Oh, man, just thinking about that marina air makes us hungry for crab sauce. Our grandfather, he didn't like taking the boat out a lot; he just liked to hang out on the docks. He had a whole patio setup and he kept a crab trap right under that boat with some chicken in it as bait. Every couple of hours, he'd check the trap and there'd be a crab or two. He'd throw 'em into this big crab pot with some onions, olive oil, salt, and pepper. It wasn't like there was a secret recipe—it was tomato sauce with crabs in it, you know? But that sauce reminded us—and still does—of a summer day. Every time we cook some up we can hear the bell on the back of the boat clangin' and smell the salt of the water.

½ cup olive oil

2 medium onions, sliced

1 tablespoon salt, plus more for the pasta water

1 teaspoon black pepper

6 cleaned blue crab claws

2 (28-ounce) cans peeled Italian tomatoes, preferably Tuttorosso or Redpack, crushed by hand

1 pound spaghetti

4 tablespoons (½ stick) salted butter

Heat the olive oil in a large pot over medium heat until shimmering. Toss in the onions, salt, and pepper along with the crabs. Sauté until the onions are caramelized. Add the tomatoes, bring the mixture to a boil, then let simmer for 1 hour. Remove the crabs from the sauce and set aside.

Meanwhile, bring a large pot of salted water to a boil. Cook the spaghetti according to the package directions until al dente, then drain and return to the pot. Add the butter, tossing until it has melted, then add the crab sauce.

Serve the crabs alongside the spaghetti so you can eat 'em with your hands.

Grandpa Dominick cooking up blue crabs

Fran and Sal out fishin'

MUSSELS AND HEINEKEN

SERVES 6 TO 8

There was nothin' we liked more than barbecuing on a sunny summer day, especially when we got older and moved outta our parents' houses. On Sundays we'd head down to Joe's Lobster House—where we bought our fish if we didn't take it from the restaurant—and go to Fran's mom's house out on the Tottenville Marina. We'd get there early, invite all our friends, and cook up a storm. We'd make so many courses it'd be like an all-day luau or clambake or somethin'. We're just like our grandfather in that way, always wantin' to feed everybody. He loved his family and wanted to make 'em food, but he also loved to do it because he loved cookin'. And he especially loved hearin' "The food's delicious" or "Wow, this was the best I ever ate."

*So we'd invite all our friends out to Fran's mom's new house that she bought in '98. It overlooked the Raritan Bay and was the second house from the beach, so you could walk outta her door and be at the water in two seconds. Fran used to play a game where he'd try to get a boat as close to the house as he could. Joy would be out there screamin', "You're gonna hit a f****** rock!"*

Usually when we made mussels at the restaurant, we'd use wine. But when there was a bunch of twenty-somethings hangin' out, we weren't drinkin' wine, we were drinkin' Heineken, so we used that instead. With all that butter and parsley and garlic, you didn't miss the wine. You could also easily substitute crab legs for an equally delicious dish.

2 tablespoons olive oil

6 garlic cloves, chopped

1 teaspoon red pepper flakes

2 tablespoons salted butter

½ bunch fresh flat-leaf parsley, leaves and stems chopped

1 teaspoon salt

3 pounds mussels, scrubbed and debearded

2 bottles warm Heineken

10 fresh basil leaves, torn

1 teaspoon dried oregano

½ lemon, for serving

In a large saucepot, heat the olive oil over medium heat. Add the garlic and red pepper flakes and cook until the garlic browns. Add the butter, parsley, salt, and mussels. When the butter has completely melted, add the Heineken and let it simmer for 3 to 5 minutes, or until the mussels open. Finish with the basil and oregano. Garnish with lemon and serve.

MUSSELS MARINARA WITH LINGUINE

SERVES 2

When you cook mussels in a pot of sauce, just openin' the lid takes you right to the marina. There was nothin' like it, especially on a Sunday afternoon in the summer. Even now it takes us right back to Grandpa Dominick's boat on the ocean. He was always cookin' mussels into the sauce, but they were more for flavor than anything else. You'd maybe get a few over your macaroni, but they weren't the main event. In the restaurant, though, that's when you got a heaping plate of mussels, like thirty, thirty-five of 'em. Mussels were cheap, so it was one of the things you could make money on in the restaurant, but they were also so delicious. And nobody really made 'em at home, so it was something special you had when you ate out.

You could eat this dish either as a starter with just the sauce and mussels or serve it over the macaroni as more of a meal. We remember our cousin Tommy would eat the mussels like he was our grandfather eatin' the pumpkin seeds (see page 92)—he'd pick all the mussels outta their shells first, put them back in the linguine, then eat the dish. It really burned Fran up; he'd sit there and seethe. The best part is sucking the mussel outta the shell with the sauce on it!

Salt

½ pound linguine

3 cups Seafood Fra Diavolo Sauce (page 143)

1 pound mussels (ideally PEI; they're the best, cleanest ones),
   scrubbed and debearded

Bring a large pot of salted water to a boil. Cook the pasta according to the package directions until al dente. Drain and set aside.

In a large saucepan, bring the sauce to a boil over high heat, add the mussels, and reduce the heat to maintain a simmer. Cook for 3 to 5 minutes or until the mussels open, discarding any that don't open. Serve as an appetizer as-is or over macaroni.

PASTA MILANESE

SERVES 4

When we were talkin' to our friend's ninety-year-old aunt about our book, she told us about some of the dishes she used to make. This one sounded like a winner, and believe us, it is.

½ cup olive oil, plus more for the pasta

6 garlic cloves

5 cans anchovies, drained

1 teaspoon red pepper flakes

3 (6-ounce) cans tomato paste,
　　such as Contadina

Salt

1 pound linguine

¼ cup Secret Bread Crumbs (page 82)

3 tablespoons grated pecorino

In a large frying pan, heat the olive oil over medium heat. Add the garlic and cook until the garlic begins to brown, then add the anchovies. Cook until the anchovies have melted into the oil, then add the red pepper flakes and tomato paste. Fill the tomato paste cans with water and add to the pan. Bring the mixture to a boil, then reduce the heat to maintain a simmer and cook for 20 minutes.

Meanwhile, bring a large pot of salted water to a boil. Add 1 teaspoon of olive oil, and cook the linguine according to the package directions until al dente. Drain and add to the pan with the sauce. Top with the bread crumbs and pecorino and serve.

RED SAUCE–STEWED CALAMARI WITH MUSSELS

SERVES 8 TO 10

If it was a Sunday, especially during Lent, Grandpa Dominick would be makin' this. Except he didn't call it anything fussy like "Red Sauce–Stewed Calamari," it was just "Hey, I made calamade." He'd cook the calamari nice and slow, which is the opposite of how most people cook it. They'll tell you that you shouldn't overcook calamari because it gets tough. But if you take it beyond that, like really cook it for a long time, it gives up. It gets real tender, like butter. Then he'd add the mussels right at the end to give it extra flavor.

3 pounds calamari, bodies and legs
   (ask your fishmonger to clean 'em)

1¾ cups olive oil

½ cup chopped garlic

¼ cup red pepper flakes

1 bunch fresh flat-leaf parsley,
   leaves and stems chopped

4 chowder or quahog clams

32 mussels, scrubbed and debearded

2 cups white wine, preferably Chardonnay

3¾ cups clam juice

4 quarts canned peeled tomatoes,
   preferably Tuttorosso or Redpack

¼ cup salt

2 tablespoons black pepper

20 fresh basil leaves

Separate the calamari legs and bodies into separate bowls. Slice the bodies into 1-inch rings and set aside.

Meanwhile, fill a small saucepan halfway with water and bring to a boil. Add the calamari legs for about 2 minutes, strain, then drain and rinse. This is to remove any ink that might be in there. Set aside.

In a large saucepot, combine the olive oil, garlic, red pepper flakes, parsley, clams, and 8 of the mussels and cook over low heat until the garlic browns.

Add the white wine and cook for 3 minutes. Add the clam juice.

Add the smashed tomatoes, the calamari rings, salt, and black pepper and cook over low heat for 1½ hours.

When there's about 10 minutes of cooking time left, add the remaining 24 mussels.

When done, remove from the heat and add the calamari legs. Finish the dish with torn basil leaves before serving.

SHRIMP TWO WAYS: MARINARA AND MILANESE

If we were cookin' shrimp at home, it was usually a holiday or Lent. It would either be butterflied, breaded, and fried, then served Grandma-style with lemon and salt, or dipped into sauce with macaroni on the side. Or it would be cooked real fast in the Seafood Fra Diavolo Sauce (page 143) and served over macaroni. We're not really sure why we called it "Shrimp Marinara," but we're guessin' it's because it sounded better than "Shrimp with Seafood Sauce." Either way, it was delicious.

SHRIMP MARINARA
SERVES 4

Salt

½ pound linguine

3 cups Seafood Fra Diavolo Sauce (page 143)

1 pound tiger shrimp, peeled with tails left on,
    deveined, and butterflied

Bring a large pot of salted water to a boil. Cook the pasta according to the package directions until al dente. Drain and set aside.

In a medium saucepan, bring the sauce to a boil, then add the shrimp and reduce the heat to maintain a simmer. Cook for 3 to 5 minutes, or until the shrimp have turned pink and opaque. Serve with the pasta.

....

SHRIMP MILANESE
SERVES 4

3 large eggs, beaten

1 cup whole milk

1 cup Dry Bread Crumbs (page 79)

1 pound tiger shrimp, peeled, deveined,
    butterflied, and pounded flat

2 cups olive oil

1 lemon, sliced into wedges

¼ head iceberg lettuce, cut into wedges

½ tomato, sliced

Tartar sauce (optional)

CONTINUED

In a large bowl, beat the eggs and milk together. Put the bread crumbs in a separate large bowl.

Dunk the shrimp into the egg mixture, then transfer them to the bowl with the bread crumbs and make sure they're completely covered. Then dunk the shrimp again into the egg mixture and back into the bread crumbs.

In a frying pan, heat the olive oil over high heat. Fry the shrimp in the hot oil until golden brown on both sides. Remove the shrimp from the pan and squeeze lemon juice over them. Serve with the lettuce wedge, tomato, and tartar sauce, if desired.

Sal's mom, Bella, in Sicily

PASTA CON SARDE

SERVES 4

A real popular holiday in the restaurant was St. Joseph's Feast. It's not as huge as Easter, but among the old-timers from Sicily, it's a big deal. Sal's mom, Bella, knew that, so she decided to do a special menu at her restaurant, Solo Bella, in Jackson, New Jersey, and donate all the money to St. Vincent's Hospital. Long story short, back in the day, there was a famine in Sicily. The villagers prayed to Saint Joseph. The famine ended, and to celebrate, they feasted. Wealthier families would put out huge buffets and invite everybody to come and eat, which is what Bella re-created in the restaurant. We're not joking when we tell you that people in their seventies and eighties would come up to our mothers with tears in their eyes saying how much this meant to them. And every year there would be a waiting list for the next March 19.

Since it fell during Lent, there was never any meat. Instead, they served lots of lentils, lots of beans, and lots of fish—peasant food. One dish in particular that was special was pasta con sarde, *or pasta with sardines, fennel, and bread crumbs. The flavors are pure Sicily, and according to Bella, the bread crumbs symbolized the sawdust from Jesus's workshop. Could also be that bread crumbs were traditionally used instead of cheese. Either way, it's a delicious dish that deserves to be eaten more than once a year.*

4 cans sardines in olive oil, oil drained
  and reserved (about 2 cups sardines)

1 white onion, sliced

1 tablespoon sliced finocchio
  (wild fennel, which is what's traditionally
  used, but regular is fine too)

¼ cup pignoli nuts

6 garlic cloves, minced

½ cup white wine

½ cup Secret Bread Crumbs (page 82)

½ cup grated pecorino

½ bunch fresh flat-leaf parsley,
  leaves and stems chopped

Salt and black pepper

1 pound spaghetti

In a medium saucepan, heat the olive oil from the sardine cans over medium heat. Add the onion, fennel, and pignoli nuts. Cook until the onion and fennel are soft, 7 to 10 minutes. Add the garlic and cook until it browns. Pour in the wine and let it boil for a couple of minutes, then add the sardines and cook until they melt, about 1 minute. Stir in the bread crumbs, cheese, and parsley. Season with salt and pepper to taste, then remove from the heat.

Bring a pot of salted water to a boil. Cook the spaghetti according to the package directions until al dente. Drain the pasta, reserving 1 cup of the cooking water.

Fold the pasta into the sardine mixture with the reserved pasta water and serve.

WHITIES WITH LEMON AND ONION

SERVES 4

Our grandfather used to fry up whiting—or "whities"—in a pan, smothered with white onions, lemon, salt, and pepper. The fish and onions were really the stars of the dish. It always made a great lunch, especially on a nice, sunny day.

1 cup olive oil

2 pounds whiting, filleted

2 cups all-purpose flour

1 white onion, sliced

1 lemon, cut into wedges

In a medium saucepan, heat the olive oil over medium-high heat. Dredge the whiting fillets evenly in the flour, then fry in the hot oil until golden brown. Serve with a garnish of raw onion and wedges of lemon.

Grandma and Grandpa's house on Thanksgiving

10

FOR HOLIDAYS 🔔 WEEKENDS

W e can't imagine a holiday without food. Or anything without food, really. It was there for the good times; it was there for the bad times. If you got a good report card, you got rewarded with food. If you were bad, you got no food. Everything was food. So on the holidays, which were such a joyous time because the whole family got together, food was an extra-big deal. You didn't make the dishes that you ate every day, and everybody did the cookin'— Aunt Loulou, Aunt Maryanne, our grandma, our moms—it was like an all-star team in the kitchen. It took real manpower to feed the army that was our family. There were friends and boyfriends and girlfriends—we're talkin' a lotta people. And of course, *everybody* loved to eat. Plus, we'd end up spendin' twelve, fourteen hours together, sometimes two days in a row. We'd go over to somebody's house for Christmas Eve and be right back over again for Christmas night. For Thanksgiving, it was the same thing, and with New Year's too. We got to see a lot of one another throughout the holiday season, and that's what made it so special.

No matter who was hosting, we'd all get there early in the mornin' so everyone could pitch in. That's also what made the holidays so great—everybody sharin' the work. Except for our cousin Nicky's wife with the long nails who'd never lift a finger, but everybody has one of those. No offense, Donna.

Even though we'd all be goin' over there to cook, there would—no matter what—already be food on the table when you got there. If you were really early, there was still breakfast out, bagels and butter and cream cheese and pastries—maybe some sticky buns or cheese buns from Andrew's, a German bakery that had the most delicious pastries you ever ate. Or if it was a little later, the table would be loaded with antipasti like cold cuts, olives, cheese, roasted peppers, bread, breadsticks, maybe some things that Grandma started cookin' the day before like stuffed mushrooms, a platter of meatballs, or eggplant. There'd already be a vat of sauce workin' on the stove, and somebody would be mannin' a frying pan, makin' like 150 cauliflower fritters that you'd be eatin' as they came outta the skillet. Then whatever was left over was piled onto a huge platter with paper towels and went onto the table.

But it wasn't like we were all sittin' around the table this whole time. You'd be outside screwin' around with your cousins or watchin' TV. If you were at Uncle Greg's you'd be in the pool, or if you were at Cousin Dom's you'd be playin' pinball in the game room. Then you'd take a break, make a plate, and go back to whatever you were doin'. But when the macaroni came out, that's when you sat down at the table. That's when things got serious. People would be walkin' outta the kitchen with two platters at a time, helpin' to serve everyone heaping plates of macaroni with sauce scooped over the top. Then came the salad, drippin' with oil and vinegar. After that was the entrées—chicken rollatini, chicken oreganata, London broil, roast beef with garlic and parsley. And after that, you got up, took a break, and maybe came back to the table for more. The women would start clearin' the dirty dishes, but the food would stay on the table. You *never* took food off the table. That was a big no-no. You didn't do it unless it was to put more food in its place.

Then there was dessert. There were things that people made, like Aunt Loulou's Rice Pudding (page 240) or Fran's mom's Icebox Cake (page 242). But no matter what, *everybody* brought somethin'. There'd be boxes and boxes of cake and cookies—rum cakes, grain cakes, cheesecakes, lobster tails, napoleons, cannoli. There'd be coffee—Italian and American—mixed with Sambuca, Frangelico, or Tia Maria, with an extra shot on the side. Everybody, the men and the women, would be smokin' cigarettes, playin' poker. Eventually the table would get filled again with dried fruit, fresh fruit, and nuts. Grandma would come out with the nutcracker and everybody would start eatin' almonds. That was what we called "dessert dessert" (see page 249). The men who did drink, that's when they started drinkin'. A popular thing was Coke mixed with red wine (see page 207). Or maybe it was Dewar's or more cordials. Then eventually your mother would start packin' up all your presents, wake you up, and drive you home.

That's what we considered normal. We never even thought that people would do things any differently. But our cousin Dom, he married a girl out in California. We remember our moms goin' out there and complainin' about how they barely served anything for dinner. "They didn't have anything out on the table when we got there!" After we moved out of Staten Island and started meeting people outside of our circles, we realized that to most people, what we do is a little nuts. But forgettaboutit—that's us.

SOPRESSATA AND PROVOLONE, HOLIDAY-STYLE

Since when did they start callin' this charcuterie? Charwhat? Charwho? To us, it was always just "sopressata and provolone," even when there were about a hundred other things on the table. Unlike regular Sopressata and Provolone (page 68), which was just for everyday company, this is a beefed-up version, because on the holidays, there's no holdin' back. This spread is also good for any party. After we moved out, there were never any Doritos or salsa and chips at our houses for watchin' the game or whatnot. It was cold cuts and cheese and olives all the way. We remember Fran's older brother comin' over once with his friends and goin', "What's wrong with you guys? You eat like old men."

There's no right or wrong way to do this. Just buy a lot of what you like and keep the food comin'.

First, there's the cold cuts: sopressata, mortadella, prosciutto, cappicola ("cappy" or "gabagool," as they call it), ham, dried sausages from the pork store (the ones hangin' from a rope over the counter; the more like leather, the better). If you don't have a good neighborhood pork store, Boar's Head makes an excellent product.

Then there's cheese. On our table it was always a soft provolone, Muenster, and pecorino that bites you back. And if we had Parmigiano-Reggiano, we'd put that out too. Set out a few big hunks and a knife and let people pick at 'em.

Now, the olives; you gotta get all different kinds—Sicilian olives, black olives, kalamata olives, olives stuffed with garlic, olives stuffed with cheese.

You could also put out the Pickled Eggplant (page 102), Eggplant Caponata (page 101), or Jay's Roasted Red Peppers (recipe follows). If you were goin' to the pork store, you could get some of the little stuffed cherry peppers or maybe the ones stuffed with prosciutto. You could even put out a can of anchovies.

And no matter what, you need some good Italian bread, like the braided loaf with sesame seeds and some seeded breadsticks.

JOY'S ROASTED RED PEPPERS

The way Fran's mother makes these is the best—she has a gas stove at home with the metal racks over the burners, and she roasts the peppers right on there. It makes the house smell mint. After that, all you have to do is add a little olive oil and some fresh garlic.

1 large red bell pepper

¼ cup olive oil

1 garlic clove, minced

2 fresh basil leaves, torn

Pinch of salt

Pinch of black pepper

Place the pepper directly over the flames on a gas stovetop burner and let it cook until the skin turns black. Rotate the pepper so that it gets evenly charred. If you don't have a gas stove, broil the pepper on a baking sheet on the top rack of your oven.

Remove it from the heat, let cool, then remove the stems, seeds, and skin, and slice it into thick pieces.

Place the pieces in a bowl, toss them with the olive oil, garlic, basil, salt, and pepper, and serve.

STUFFED ARTICHOKES

SERVES 6

As kids, we always loved these. They were something that we had on holidays, especially Easter. All our aunts and our moms and our grandmother made 'em exactly the same way—stuffed with bread crumbs and grated cheese, and sometimes with pignoli nuts to make 'em a little fancier. They took a long time to make and called for a good amount of prep, but for special occasions, it was really worth it. So worth it that we named our pizzeria after the things. In the beginning, we wouldn't even open the doors to the store if the stuffed artichokes weren't ready and on the counter. After all, the name of the place is "Artichoke"—how could we not have the best stuffed artichokes in the city? We needed at least two big trays' worth because they went so fast. No one had ever sold 'em like that before, like fast food, and people went nuts for 'em. No kidding!

3 cups Secret Bread Crumbs (page 82)

½ cup pignoli nuts

4 cups chicken broth

½ cup olive oil

6 garlic cloves, minced

½ bunch fresh flat-leaf parsley, finely chopped

6 whole artichokes, rinsed

1 lemon, cut into wedges, for serving

Preheat the oven to 425°F.

In a medium bowl, mix the bread crumbs and pignoli nuts until well blended. Reserve 1 cup of the mixture in a separate bowl. Set aside.

In a separate bowl, combine the chicken broth, olive oil, garlic, and parsley.

Trim the stems off the bottom of the artichokes and trim about 3 inches from the top (so almost half is trimmed off).

Stuff the bread crumb mixture between the artichoke leaves as tightly as possible. Arrange the artichokes in a deep baking dish or roasting pan, then pour the chicken broth dressing into the bottom of the pan. It should come about halfway up the sides of the artichokes.

CONTINUED

Cover the dish with foil and transfer to the oven. Cook for 1 hour, then remove the foil and cook, uncovered, for 15 minutes more, or until the artichokes and stuffing are golden brown. Before eating, ladle a little of the reserved stuffing over the artichokes. Serve with lemon wedges.

WHAT WE WERE DRINKIN'

The people in our family weren't really big drinkers, but when they did drink, it was usually one of two things—Dewar's or Coke and red wine.

DEWAR'S

In our family, Dewar's is pretty much everybody's drink. Fran remembers our grandmother teachin' him to drink it. There was a time when we were runnin' around to all the bars, drinkin' just about anything—tequila, Absolut and cranberry, all that stupid stuff—until our grandmother straightened us out. It was Fran's mother's fiftieth-birthday party, and Fran got so sick off Cuervo that he ended up lyin' on the bathroom floor, his face on the cold tile. Our grandmother, she pulled him aside and said, "You drink that shit, you're gonna feel like shit the next day. Dewar's on the rocks is what you drink. You won't get all sick and stupid." It wasn't fashionable, especially for a twenty-one-year-old, and bartenders would look at him like he had nine heads when he ordered it—then go dust off the one bottle they had—but Grandma was right. To this day, it's all Fran drinks.

COKE AND RED WINE

Nothin' much to it.

½ cup Coca-Cola
½ cup red wine, preferably Carlo Rossi Paisano

Mix equal parts Coke and wine; serve with one ice cube.

❧

JEWISH ROMAN ARTICHOKES, TWICE FRIED

SERVES 4

When we opened Artichoke, we wanted to add more artichoke items to the menu, so we came up with this simple dish. All you do is take artichoke hearts with a little bit of stem attached, cook 'em in oil over a low flame until they're almost completely cooked, drain 'em, then turn up the heat real high and hot and crisp 'em up. Sprinkle 'em with salt and pepper and serve 'em right outta the fryer. People will lose their minds.

12 fresh baby artichokes

1 cup olive oil

½ tablespoon sea salt

Trim the stems where they meet the base of the artichokes. Then, holding them sideways, trim about 2 inches off the top of the artichokes. Next, peel the leaves off each artichoke until you get to the pale green leaves—the artichoke should look like a pale green rose. Halve the artichokes lengthwise.

In a medium saucepan, heat the olive oil over medium heat. Add the artichokes and fry, turning occasionally to cook both sides, for 5 to 7 minutes, or until fork-tender. Transfer the artichokes to a paper towel.

Turn the heat up to high, then place the artichokes back in the pan and flash-fry them for about a minute to crisp them. Remove from the pan, sprinkle with the sea salt, and serve immediately.

SUNDAY GRAVY WITH BRACIOLE

SERVES 8

We've heard a lot of people make the argument that the difference between sauce *and* gravy *is that gravy is made with meat. Most of the time on Sundays when we're makin' a pot of sauce, it not only has the neck bones like in a regular cooked sauce, it also has braciole—or pork cutlets stuffed with hard-boiled eggs, salami, cheese, garlic, and parsley. That's what really flavors the sauce, because it's simmerin' in there for hours. Then when you're done, you don't even need a knife, because the meat is so tender it just falls apart.*

Even though it's sort of its own dish, braciole is really a part of the sauce. It was never like, "Oh, I'm havin' braciole today." It's just gravy. And when it came time to eat, you got the macaroni and sauce first, then the meat came out second.

For the Braciole:

8 pork cutlets (about 2 pounds)

8 hard-boiled eggs, sliced

8 slices Genoa salami

4 teaspoons minced garlic

4 teaspoons chopped fresh flat-leaf parsley

½ cup grated pecorino

Salt and black pepper

1¾ cups olive oil

2½ Spanish onions, finely chopped

For the Gravy:

3 beef short rib bones

3 pork neck bones

4 quarts peeled tomatoes, preferably Tuttorosso or Redpack

1 (56-ounce) can tomato puree, preferably Suzy Bell

2 pounds rigatoni, cooked

NOTE: Have butcher rope or kitchen twine ready.

MAKE THE BRACIOLE:

Cover the cutlets with plastic wrap and pound with a skillet or mallet until about ¼ inch thick. Divide the eggs, salami, garlic, parsley, and cheese evenly among the cutlets. Add a dash of salt and pepper. Roll up each cutlet like a cigar and use butcher rope or kitchen twine to secure the rolls. We recommend using three pieces—one in the middle and one at each end of the cutlet.

CONTINUED

In a large saucepot, heat the olive oil over medium heat. Add the cutlet rolls and sear until lightly browned on each side, 2 to 3 minutes. Add the onions, season with salt and pepper, and sauté until the onions brown, 10 to 15 minutes.

Remove the braciole from the pot and set aside.

MAKE THE GRAVY:

Add the bones to the pot in which you cooked the braciole and turn the heat down to low. Allow the bones to render for about 15 minutes, stirring occasionally.

Meanwhile, in a large bowl, smash the peeled tomatoes by hand until they're a chunky consistency. Add the smashed tomatoes and tomato puree to the pot, return the braciole to the pot, and simmer for 2 hours, stirring every 5 minutes.

To serve, first put out the rigatoni. Then remove the braciole from the sauce, cut off the string, and heap onto a plate.

GRANDMA'S MEATBALLS

MAKES ABOUT 15 MEATBALLS

These meatballs were a lot like the eggplant—they were always around. Every Sunday, if there was a pot of sauce on the stove, these would be in a fryin' pan. There's not much about 'em that's different from your standard-issue meatball, but then again, Grandma put enough garlic in 'em to give you agita for three days. Because she mixed the garlic in raw instead of browning it first, it was heartburn city—in the best possible way. There was so much flavor. She also never made 'em with all meat, the way a lotta people make 'em now. Back in the day, when times were bad, you needed bread crumbs to stretch the meat. You could turn 2 pounds of meat into 4 pounds of food. But it also makes for a more balanced meatball. Just because you can afford to make 'em with all meat doesn't mean it's the way to go. To us, it's like eatin' a ball of flavored hamburger. Maybe it's just what we're used to, but we think it's better with bread crumbs. Or if you don't have bread crumbs, you can use sliced bread instead, which is what our grandma sometimes did. Just soak 4 slices of white bread like Wonder Bread in water and squeeze out the excess liquid.

Grandma Connie in the original Chubby Mary's

In this version of the recipe we call for baking the meatballs instead of frying them because it's easier—it's how we did it in the restaurant. That way, you don't have to stand over a hot pan all afternoon. But if you'd rather fry 'em, just heat 2 cups of olive oil in a large frying pan and cook the meatballs until they're golden brown, 2 to 3 minutes a side.

Last, if you don't have cooked sauce prepared already, and are making it along with your meatballs, all you have to do is simmer the meatballs in the sauce for the last hour of the cook time after they've been browned.

CONTINUED

FOR HOLIDAYS AND WEEKENDS

1 cup Secret Bread Crumbs (page 82), or 4 slices white bread soaked in water

1 pound ground beef

1 pound ground pork

3 large eggs

1 cup grated pecorino

1½ teaspoons salt

Black pepper

6 garlic cloves, chopped

6 sprigs fresh flat-leaf parsley, leaves and stems chopped

1 recipe Cooked Sauce (page 141)

Preheat the oven to 350°F.

Line a rimmed baking pan with aluminum foil. Combine all the ingredients except the cooked sauce in a large bowl and mix with your hands, being careful not to overmix. If the mixture is too dry, add water in ¼-cup increments.

Roll the mixture into golf ball–size balls or ovals and place them in the lined baking pan.

Add ¼ cup water to the pan and carefully transfer to the oven. Bake for 1 hour, or until the meatballs are golden brown. Remove and set aside.

When the meatballs are almost done, place the sauce in a large pot and heat through. When the oil turns dark and rises to the top of the tomato sauce, add the baked meatballs and cook for about 1 hour.

Serve over pasta, on a sandwich, or on the side.

TONY SCOTTO'S PIGNOLI-RAISIN MEATBALLS

MAKES 15 MEATBALLS

Tony Scotto was like an uncle to Fran, even though they weren't blood related. Growin' up, he was Fran's mother's brother's best friend, so he was like part of the family. They even called him Uncle Tony. Fran wanted to be him when he was younger—like Uncle Gregory, he was the epitome of cool. He owned a million-dollar business called Island Patio that sold aboveground pools and patio furniture, and he did some construction too. He had a white Lincoln Continental, beautiful clothes, beautiful jewelry. He knew how to make money, and he knew how to spend it. After Fran's dad moved out, he didn't see him so much because he eventually had another family. But Tony Scotto, he came over to the house all the time. For years he came every Sunday. He and his wife had gotten divorced, so Fran's mom brought him around to be part of her group of single friends. And most of all, he was a role model for Fran. He was always telling him to do this or that and makin' him work at his fencing yard. But he and Fran's mom never dated, even though they were so close. Because like we said, he was family. And like family, we were always happy to cook something special for him. So when he asked Joy to make these meatballs that his mother would make for him—and that were one of his favorite things—she happily did.

These are just like Grandma's Meatballs, only they have raisins and pignoli nuts and they never get cooked in sauce. They just get fried and put on a paper towel and are served just like that, usually as an appetizer on Sundays or holidays.

1 recipe Grandma's Meatballs
   (page 213), uncooked
1 cup pignoli nuts
1 cup raisins

Follow the recipe for Grandma's Meatballs on page 213, but add the pignoli nuts and raisins. Bake as directed, but skip cooking the meatballs in the sauce. Serve without sauce.

CHICKEN OREGANATA

SERVES 4

This is a nice, light dish that was usually one of the meats on the table when the family got together on a Sunday. It was great for feeding a lotta people because you set up the chicken cutlets over butter, lemon, and chicken stock, top the dish off with some tomatoes and bread crumbs, garlic, and parsley, then put it in the oven and could get back to something else. The top gets all crispy and delicious like a baked clam, while the juices in the pan keep the meat real tender. If you gotta cook for twenty people and need a one-pan deal, this is the way to go.

2 chicken cutlets

1 teaspoon salt

1 teaspoon black pepper

1 tablespoon salted butter,
    at room temperature

½ cup white wine

1½ cups chicken stock

3 tablespoons olive oil

1 tablespoon minced garlic

1 tablespoon chopped fresh flat-leaf parsley

1 whole tomato, cut into ¼-inch-thick rounds

2 cups Secret Bread Crumbs (page 82)

1 lemon, for serving

Preheat the oven to 450°F.

Season the chicken cutlets with the salt and pepper. Coat the bottom of a rimmed baking sheet with the butter and arrange the chicken on top. Add the wine, chicken stock, olive oil, garlic, and parsley, then cover the chicken with the tomato rounds. Top the tomatoes evenly with the bread crumbs. Cover the baking sheet with foil and roast for 15 to 20 minutes. Remove the foil and roast for an additional 3 minutes to brown the bread crumbs. Serve immediately with a squeeze of fresh lemon juice.

STUFFED SHELLS

SERVES 6

There's nothing to this dish but big Ronzoni shells filled with ricotta and grated cheese, smothered in sauce, and baked in the oven. It's perfect for the kids at Christmas or Thanksgiving.

Salt

1 pound large shells, preferably Ronzoni

4 cups ricotta

1 cup grated pecorino

3 cups Cooked Sauce (page 141)

1 cup shredded mozzarella

1 teaspoon finely chopped fresh flat-leaf parsley

Preheat the oven to 450°F.

Bring a large pot of salted water to a boil. Cook the pasta according to the package directions until al dente, stirring gently so the shells do not break. Carefully drain the pasta and set aside to cool.

Stuff each shell with about 1 tablespoon of the ricotta and a sprinkle of pecorino.

Spread a thin layer of sauce over the bottom of a medium baking pan. Place the stuffed shells in the pan and cover them generously with tomato sauce. Scatter the mozzarella over the top—so there's about a tablespoon on each shell—and sprinkle the remaining pecorino over the top. Cook the shells for 5 to 7 minutes, or until the cheese has completely melted. Sprinkle with parsley and serve.

CHICKEN ROLLATINI

SERVES 4

This was a Saturday night kind of dish. It took a little longer than a fast-and-easy weeknight meal, but man, was it delicious. First, we stuffed some chicken cutlets with ham, cheese, and parsley, then we floured 'em, fried 'em, baked 'em with some chicken broth to make 'em extra juicy, then smothered 'em in marsala wine sauce.

For the Chicken:

4 chicken cutlets

Salt and black pepper

4 thin slices ham

2 slices mozzarella

2 tablespoons grated pecorino

1 teaspoon finely chopped
   fresh flat-leaf parsley

Flour for dredging

2 cups olive oil

1 cup chicken broth

For the Marsala Sauce:

½ teaspoon all-purpose flour

1 tablespoon plus ½ teaspoon
   salted butter

1 tablespoon olive oil

½ white onion, quartered

6 cremini mushrooms, sliced

Pinch of red pepper flakes

Salt and black pepper

½ cup marsala wine

2 cups chicken broth

½ cup beef broth

MAKE THE CHICKEN:

Preheat the oven to 400°F.

Cover the cutlets with plastic wrap and pound them with a mallet or the bottom of a frying pan to ½- to ¼-inch thickness. Take 2 of the cutlets and lay them side by side so they form 1 large cutlet. Do the same with the other 2 cutlets so you now have 2 very large cutlets.

Lightly season the chicken with salt and pepper. Place 2 slices of the ham, a slice of the mozzarella, and half the pecorino and parsley on top of each cutlet. Next, roll up each cutlet like a burrito. Dredge the rolled cutlets evenly in the flour.

In a small frying pan, heat the olive oil over medium-high heat. Fry the rolled cutlets for about 3 minutes a side, or until lightly golden. Transfer the chicken from the pan to a small baking dish.

CONTINUED

Add 1 cup of chicken broth to the baking dish and bake for 10 to 15 minutes, or until the chicken is cooked through. You can cut off a piece of the chicken to make sure it's fully cooked. There should be no pink in the meat; it should be white all the way through.

MAKE THE MARSALA SAUCE:

While the chicken is baking, make a roux, or a combination of equal parts flour and butter, which thickens the sauce. All you have to do is mix together ½ teaspoon of flour and ½ teaspoon of butter. Set aside.

In a medium saucepan, combine the olive oil, remaining 1 tablespoon butter, the onion, and the mushrooms. Sauté the mixture over medium heat until the onion begins to soften, about 5 minutes. Add a pinch of red pepper flakes, salt, and black pepper. Pour in the marsala, chicken broth, and beef broth and bring to a boil. Cook for 3 to 5 minutes at a boil, which will cook out the wine.

Add the roux while whisking rapidly until the sauce gets thick. Remove the pot from the heat and serve the sauce over the chicken, or any pasta.

CHICKEN FRANCESE

SERVES 4

Just like Chicken Rollatini (page 221), this dish usually showed up on Saturdays in our house. But the place we cooked it the most was in the restaurant. It's a real popular entrée in Italian restaurants, and you'll even see it in hero shops. When we did parties in our event space upstairs we'd give people a choice of dinner dish. And outta the chickens—parmigiana, marsala, or Francese—everybody would get the Francese. We'd literally be standin' back there in the kitchen makin' chicken Francese for fifty people. Basically, you just flour the chicken, crack a coupla eggs, mix 'em with grated cheese, parsley, salt, and pepper, then coat the chicken and fry it. It's almost like egg foo yong the way the exterior is sorta eggy and soaks up all the sauce, which is just white wine, butter, and lemon, so it's got a little bright flavor to it. That gets poured right over the top, and that's it. Perfect.

1 cup all-purpose flour

Salt and black pepper

6 large eggs

½ cup olive oil

8 chicken cutlets

1 cup chicken broth

1 cup white wine, preferably Chardonnay

Juice of 2 lemons, plus 1 lemon, sliced

2 tablespoons unsalted butter

¼ cup finely chopped fresh
    flat-leaf parsley leaves and stems

Place the flour in a medium bowl and season with salt and pepper. In a separate medium bowl, beat the eggs. Set aside.

Heat the olive oil in a large frying pan over medium heat.

Dredge each chicken cutlet in the flour, then soak it in the egg. Fry the chicken in the hot oil until golden brown, 8 to 10 minutes a side. Transfer to a plate.

In a large saucepan, combine the chicken broth and wine and bring to a boil. Reduce the heat to maintain a simmer and add the lemon juice. Put the chicken in the saucepan and add the butter. Cook for 3 minutes more, or until the sauce saturates the chicken.

Serve the chicken with extra sauce poured over the top, a sprinkling of parsley, and a couple of slices of lemon.

CHICKEN À LA JENNI

SERVES 2

A friend of ours we went to high school with, Mike, his mom always dreamed of opening a restaurant. She was this big woman—the whole family was big—and she loved to cook and feed people. Well, one day she moved down to Florida, got remarried to a man from there—you know, a real swamp guy with a pontoon boat, overalls, and whatnot—and made it happen. We'd go out there and visit Mike, and she'd make us this dish. You know shrimp toast from a Chinese restaurant? This was like that. It was chicken rollatini stuffed with mushrooms and onions and muzzarell, but the twist was that she breaded 'em with slices of Wonder Bread, then deep-fried the whole thing. It had that spongy, golden shrimp toast effect on the outside and on the inside the chicken was cooked perfectly, with the juices all locked in. We wanted to put it on our mothers' menu but Fran's mother kept saying, "It's too greasy; you're gonna kill somebody with that thing!" But we think it's an excellent dish.

For the Chicken:

2 tablespoons salted butter

1½ cups button mushrooms, finely chopped

1 medium onion, finely chopped

1 tablespoon finely chopped fresh flat-leaf parsley

1 teaspoon salt

½ teaspoon black pepper

½ cup dry white wine

2 large chicken breasts, pounded to a ¼-inch thickness

¼ cup shredded mozzarella cheese

All-purpose flour

3 large eggs

1 cup whole milk

6 slices Wonder Bread, crusts removed

2 cups olive oil

For the Sauce:

2 tablespoons olive oil

2 tablespoons chopped onion

1 teaspoon chopped garlic

2 button mushrooms, sliced

¼ cup diced fresh tomato

½ cup white wine

1½ cups heavy cream

1 tablespoon salted butter

1 teaspoon salt

½ teaspoon black pepper

MAKE THE CHICKEN:

In a frying pan, combine the butter, mushrooms, onion, parsley, salt, and pepper. Cook over medium heat until the onions are caramelized. Add the white wine and let it cook off almost completely.

Lay the chicken breasts on a flat surface and spoon about 5 tablespoons of the sautéed mixture on the center of each. Divide the mozzarella evenly between the 2 breasts. Roll each breast into a rollatini. Dredge the rollatini in flour and set aside.

Preheat the oven to 500°F.

Beat the eggs and milk together in a bowl. Dip the floured rollatini into the egg mixture and coat well. Then wrap each rollatini entirely with 3 slices of bread: one on top, one on the bottom, and a half on each side. The bread might not cooperate with you, but do the best you can. Use more egg to help the bread stick, if necessary.

Heat the oil in a small saucepan over medium-high heat. Fry the rollatini in the hot oil until deep golden brown, 3 to 4 minutes on each side.

Transfer the rollatini to a baking sheet and bake for at least 20 minutes. Slice a rollatini in half to test for doneness—the meat should be completely white with no traces of pink.

MAKE THE SAUCE:

In a frying pan, heat the olive oil over medium heat. Add the onion and cook until softened, about 3 minutes. Add the garlic, mushrooms, tomato, and wine. Let cook for 2 minutes, then add the heavy cream, butter, salt, and pepper. Lower the flame and let the sauce reduce while whisking until it becomes creamy. Pour over chicken and serve.

BABY MEATBALL AND BONE SOUP WITH ESCAROLE

(ITALIAN WEDDING SOUP)

SERVES 6 TO 8

We never actually called this "Italian Wedding Soup," and we're not sure if this is really what you'd eat at an Italian wedding, but we do know that it is one delicious dish. Our grandma made it on weekends because it'd take some time to roll out all the little meatballs. She'd cook them first, then make a bone broth with carrots, celery, and onions—which would get just the right amount of grease from the bones—and add in some tomatoes and escarole. Then she'd serve it with pasta or rice and grated cheese.

½ cup olive oil

2 white onions, cut into wedges

1 pound beef short ribs

1 pound beef neck bones

¼ cup salt

2 tablespoons black pepper

2 cups Cooked Sauce (page 141)

1 batch Grandma's Meatballs (page 213), uncooked, rolled into tablespoon-size balls

3 heads escarole, rinsed well and chopped

1 pound ditalini

In a large saucepot, heat the olive oil over medium heat. Add the onions and sauté until soft, 3 to 4 minutes. Add the short ribs, neck bones, salt, and pepper and cook for 15 minutes. Add the sauce and sauté for 5 minutes more.

Pour in 16 cups water and bring the liquid to a boil. Add the meatballs and cook for 30 minutes, then add the escarole, cooking just until it gets soft, 2 to 3 minutes. Keep the mixture at a boil and add the pasta. Cook according to the package directions until the pasta is al dente. Serve.

Cousin Gasper, Uncle JoJo, Great-Grandpa Gregory,

11

AS IF WE REALLY NEED IT

· DESSERTS ·

There's one person who comes to mind when we think of dessert, and that's our great-grandfather Gregory Auditorre. He came here as a baker from Italy and opened two pastry shops in Brooklyn. They were pretty popular and have a very impressive legacy. There's an institution in Carroll Gardens called Court Pastry on Court Street that's seriously the Holy Grail of Italian cookies. The guy who owns it, Gasper Zerilli, he worked for our great-grandfather and makes the same treats that we would eat growin' up from Great-Grandpa Gregory's shop—cannolis, *sfogliatelle, saviata,* anisette cookies, lemon drops, twist cookies. There's even a picture of our great-grandfather on the wall.

Our great-grandfather wasn't just a great baker, though—the guy also loved to paint. One of his bakeries was named Mona Lisa, and he did all kinds of renditions of the famous painting—Mona Lisa lookin' at the *Mona Lisa*, Mona Lisa with cats. It was odd, but it was creative. He put his own spin on it, you know? He did a big mural in our uncle Pudgie's place in Miami, Casale's Alley, and his painting of the three Kennedy brothers is still hangin' in all our restaurants. He had a coupla exhibits in the sixties in Manhattan, and when he retired from the pastry shop, he took up painting full-time.

··································

Sal's mom, Bella, in Basille's, Middletown, New Jersey

UNCLE FRANKIE'S "S" COOKIES

MAKES 12 TO 16 COOKIES

As we mentioned before, our uncle Frankie was nuts (more on this on page 47). He had a million cats and was always screamin' at them, callin' 'em all kinds of names that we couldn't print here. But it's because of him that our great-grandfather's pastries live on in our family. Uncle Frankie, crazy as he mighta been, re-created a lot of Great-Grandpa Gregory's delicious recipes, especially these "S" cookies.

These are a little sweet and a little dry, makin' 'em perfect for dippin' into coffee. When Uncle Frankie made them, they always had cat hair in 'em, and maybe that was the secret ingredient, but we wouldn't recommend it.

4 cups all-purpose flour

1 tablespoon baking powder

¾ teaspoon baking soda

2½ cups granulated sugar

5 large eggs

1 cup (2 sticks) salted butter, melted

1½ tablespoons vanilla extract

Juice of ½ lemon

Preheat the oven to 350°F.

In a large bowl or the bowl of a stand mixer fitted with the whisk attachment, whisk together the flour, baking powder, baking soda, and sugar until well combined.

Add the eggs, butter, vanilla, and lemon juice and blend until the batter is evenly mixed.

Transfer the batter to a large piping bag fitted with a large plain tip. Pipe out 3-inch-long "S" shapes onto a large nonstick baking sheet.

Bake the cookies for 10 minutes, or until golden brown. Let cool on the baking sheet before serving.

LEMON DROPS

MAKES 24 COOKIES

This was one of the biggest sellers at our great-grandfather's shop, and it was something that was always on the table. If you were havin' company, you got a box of lemon drops and put them out with dessert and coffee. When you go to Court Pastry, they have these in abundance, and we highly recommend you try theirs or make your own. Even though our great-grandfather would never use a mix, we found it's an easy way to get a great product if you don't have a lot of baking experience.

For the Cookies:

1 box lemon cake mix

2 large eggs

⅓ cup vegetable oil

2 teaspoons freshly grated lemon zest

¼ cup confectioners' sugar

For the Glaze:

1½ cups confectioners' sugar

MAKE THE COOKIES:

Preheat the oven to 375°F.

In a large bowl, combine the cake mix, eggs, oil, and lemon zest until well blended.

Place the confectioners' sugar in a wide bowl. Using a tablespoon, drop the batter in tablespoon-size dollops into the sugar and roll them around gently with your hand or a spoon to coat generously.

Transfer the sugar-coated dollops to a large nonstick baking sheet and bake for 8 to 10 minutes, or until golden brown.

MAKE THE GLAZE:

In a small bowl, whisk together the confectioners' sugar and 3 tablespoons water until the mixture has the consistency of pancake batter. Add a little more water if necessary.

When the cookies have cooled, submerge them in the glaze and lay them on waxed paper until the glaze hardens.

SAVIATA

MAKES 12 TO 16 COOKIES

Saviata, or Italian ladyfingers, are one of the best things you could eat, especially dipped into milk or coffee until they get all soggy. They're a little dry, so they act like a sponge when you dunk 'em. The key is a batter that's a lot looser than regular cookie batter and baking at a low heat.

6 large eggs

1½ cups granulated sugar

1 cup vegetable oil

2 tablespoons vanilla extract

3½ cups all-purpose flour

2 tablespoons baking powder

¼ cup confectioners' sugar

Preheat the oven to 300°F.

In a large bowl, combine the eggs, granulated sugar, oil, and vanilla. Add the flour and baking powder and mix well.

Place the confectioners' sugar in a medium bowl.

Form 3-inch-long biscuits of batter with your hands and dip them into the confectioners' sugar to cover thoroughly. Place the cookies on a large nonstick baking sheet and bake for 15 to 20 minutes, or until the cookies are just set. They should still be white. Let cool to room temperature before serving.

PIGNOLI COOKIES

MAKES 12 COOKIES

There's probably not one Staten Islander who doesn't know about a pignoli cookie. They're a real popular Italian cookie and aren't hard to make. We'd usually only have 'em on holidays because the pignolis are a little expensive, but these are to die for. They're not a coffee cookie like a twist cookie or an "S" cookie that you can dip and eat; they're sweet and soft—almost like a little almond-and-rum-flavored soufflé.

3 large egg whites

1 cup granulated sugar

10 ounces almond paste, crumbled

5 ounces pignoli nuts

Preheat the oven to 350°F.

In a medium bowl or the bowl of a stand mixer fitted with the paddle attachment, beat together the egg whites and sugar. Work in the almond paste crumbles. Whip the mixture until the consistency is even and smooth.

Spread the pignoli nuts on a flat surface and use a tablespoon to dollop the dough mixture on top. Transfer the cookies nut-side up to a non-stick baking sheet, keeping the cookies at least 2 inches from each other.

Bake for 15 to 20 minutes, or until golden brown. Let cool completely before serving.

RICE PUDDING

SERVES 8

Aunt Loulou was the rice pudding queen in the family. Our grandmother made it, our grandfather made it, but when we think of rice pudding, it's Aunt Loulou's all the way. Anytime you went over to her house, she was like Grandma and the eggplant—there was always rice puddin' on the table. She used to make a giant pot of it, package it into these little plastic cups with cinnamon, and sell 'em at Uncle Greg's hero shops. Everybody knew that Greg's in downtown Brooklyn on Van Brunt Street had the best rice pudding, and everybody wanted to know what her recipe was, but she wouldn't tell a soul. For a long time, not even her twin sister, Gilda, knew what the big secret was. Then years ago, when our aunt Loulou and Gilda were helpin' us out at the restaurant, Gilda spilled the beans. She goes, "Oh yeah, you gotta use the half-and-half." We remember Loulou shootin' her the dirtiest look.

It's true, though—heavy cream made it too creamy and regular milk wasn't creamy enough. It was the half-and-half that got it to just the right consistency. Of course, that wasn't the only thing to it. You gotta cook the rice just right and add the perfect amount of vanilla and cinnamon.

4 cups half-and-half

2 cups long-grain white rice, such as Carolina

½ cup granulated sugar

1 large egg, beaten

1 teaspoon vanilla extract

2 tablespoons ground cinnamon

In a medium saucepan, combine the half-and-half and rice and bring to a boil. Reduce the heat to low and simmer for 20 minutes. Stir in the sugar and egg and cook for 2 to 3 minutes more, then stir in the vanilla. Remove from the heat and let cool completely. Top with the cinnamon and serve.

ICEBOX CAKE

SERVES 12

One time, Fran's mother's best friend, Roseanne, who, of course, lived down the block, made an icebox cake and brought it over. We were like, "What the hell is this? It's so thin and so dry." Fran's mom told us to shut up, but we knew good icebox cake when we saw it. Roseanne, she made it cheap. She only used one box of pudding mix instead of four, and it definitely wasn't My-T-Fine pudding mix, which was all our aunts or grandparents ever used. Jell-O didn't cut the mustard in our house.

Icebox cake was something that we ate on holidays, and most of the time you had your pick— our aunt Loulou's or Fran's mother's. They'd be in these enormous catering pans because these cakes were six, eight inches thick, layered with graham crackers and chocolate and vanilla pudding. Aunt Loulou and Joy were always tryin' to one-up each other with how big their cakes were. The one rule they had was that you never, ever use low-fat or skim milk. It would make the cake more firm and easier to cut, but it would suck. It had to be whole milk. Icebox cake pretty much looks like slop when you cut into it, but it's outta this world. Serve it up cold, stick a spoon in it, and dig in.

4 (3-ounce) boxes My-T-Fine
    chocolate pudding mix

4 (3-ounce) boxes My-T-Fine
    vanilla pudding mix

1 gallon whole milk

2 boxes Nabisco Graham Crackers,
    crumbled

2 cups heavy cream

Granulated sugar

Follow the directions on the packages for making the pudding, using as much milk as needed. Set aside.

In the bottom of the baking dish, spread a layer of graham cracker crumbles. Cover with a layer of vanilla pudding, followed by another layer of graham cracker crumbles, and then a layer of chocolate pudding. Continue alternating until you reach the top of the pan, ending with a pudding layer. Cover and refrigerate for at least 4 hours before serving.

When ready to serve, whip the heavy cream, adding sugar to taste, and dollop the whipped cream on top of the cake.

PASTEIS DE NATA

(PORTUGUESE EGG CUSTARD TARTS)

MAKES ABOUT 40 PASTRIES

Aunt Tina (remember, the one who made the Chicken and Lard on page 164?), she also made this dish, and we'd put it up there in the same category as cauliflower fritters in terms of deliciousness and awesomeness. They're basically hand-size egg custard tarts. Like a flan, but better. We don't know how these things aren't all over. How is there not a guy in Manhattan only sellin' these? He'd make a fortune! Maybe it's something we should think about…

For the Dough:

2 cups all-purpose flour, plus more for
    rolling out the dough

¼ teaspoon sea salt

1 cup (2 sticks) unsalted butter,
    at room temperature, whipped until
    smooth in a stand mixer or in a bowl
    with a spatula

For the Custard:

3 tablespoons all-purpose flour

1¼ cups whole milk

1⅓ cups granulated sugar

1 cinnamon stick

½ teaspoon pure vanilla extract

6 large egg yolks, whisked

For Assembly:

Salted butter, for the pan

Confectioners' sugar

Ground cinnamon

MAKE THE DOUGH:

In the bowl of a stand mixer fitted with the dough hook, mix the flour, salt, and 1 cup water until a soft, pillowy dough comes together, about 30 seconds.

Turn out the dough onto a floured work surface and pat it into a 6-inch square using a pastry scraper as a guide. Flour the dough, cover with plastic wrap, and let rest for 15 minutes.

CONTINUED

Roll the dough into an 18-inch square using the scraper to lift the dough every now and then to make sure it's not sticking. Brush the excess flour off the top, trim any uneven edges, and, using a small spatula, dot and then spread the left two-thirds of the dough with a little less than one-third of the butter. Leave 1 inch at the edge unbuttered.

Carefully fold over the unbuttered right third of the dough (using the pastry scraper to loosen it if it sticks), brush off any excess flour, then fold over the left third. Starting from the top, pat down the dough packet with your hand to release air bubbles, then pinch the edges closed. Brush off any excess flour.

Turn the dough packet 90 degrees to the left so the fold is facing you. Lift the packet and flour the work surface below. Once again roll the dough out into an 18-inch square, then spread the left two-thirds of the dough with another one-third of the butter, leaving 1 inch unbuttered at the edge. Fold as you did before.

For the last rolling, turn the packet 90 degrees to the left and roll out the dough into an 18 x 21-inch rectangle. Adjust it so the shorter edge is facing you. Spread the remaining butter over the entire surface. Using a spatula as an aid, lift the edge closest to you and roll the dough away from you into a tight log, brushing the excess flour from the underside as you go. Trim the ends and cut the log in half. Wrap each piece in plastic wrap and chill overnight.

MAKE THE CUSTARD:

In a medium bowl, whisk together the flour and $\frac{1}{4}$ cup of the milk until smooth. Set aside.

In a small saucepan, combine the granulated sugar, cinnamon stick, and $\frac{2}{3}$ cup water and bring to a boil. Cook until the mixture registers 200°F on an instant-read thermometer. Do not stir. Remove from the heat.

In a separate small saucepan, scald the remaining 1 cup milk over low heat. Whisk the hot milk into the flour mixture. Remove the cinnamon stick from the sugar mixture and pour the syrup in a thin stream into the hot milk and flour mixture, whisking briskly. Add the vanilla and stir for a minute until the mixture is very warm, but not hot. Whisk in the yolks, strain the custard through a fine-mesh strainer into a bowl, cover with plastic wrap, and set aside.

ASSEMBLE THE PASTRIES:

Preheat the oven to 500°F. Butter the wells of a muffin tin.

Remove the pastry log from the refrigerator and roll it back and forth on a lightly floured surface with your hands until it's about 1 inch in diameter and 16 inches long. Cut the log into ¾-inch pieces and place them cut-side down in each well of the muffin pan.

Allow the dough pieces to rest for a few minutes until they're pliable. Have a small cup of water nearby. Dip your thumbs into the water, then straight down into the middle of the dough spiral. Flatten the dough against the bottom of the well so it's about ⅛ inch thick, then smooth the dough up the sides of the pan to create a raised lip that's about ⅛ inch above the pan. The pastry sides should be thinner than the bottom. Repeat with the remaining dough. Fill each dough cup three-quarters full with the slightly warm custard.

Bake until the edges of the dough are golden brown, 8 to 9 minutes. Remove from the oven and let cool for a few minutes in the pan. Transfer to a rack and let cool until just warm. Sprinkle the pastries with confectioners' sugar, then cinnamon, and serve.

The pastries can be refrigerated for up to 3 days, and the dough can be frozen for a couple of months.

SAL THE BAKER'S FRUIT TART

MAKES 2 TARTS

There was a guy who lived on our block whose name was Sal the Baker. Picture a big Italian guy who looked like a "Sal the Baker," mustache and all. That was him. Had a real pretty Italian wife too. We used to hang out on his fence because one of our friends lived next door, and Sal the Baker would always say "You're gonna break my fence!" Anyway, he had a pastry shop called Alta Pastry in Staten Island, which had great pastries. Everything there was good, but the best by far were his fruit tarts, which were filled with custard and had fruit layered on top. We could never just buy one tart, so this recipe makes two.

2½ cups whole milk

¼ cup all-purpose flour

¼ cup granulated sugar

3 large egg yolks

2 teaspoons freshly grated lemon zest

1 teaspoon vanilla extract

4 cups strawberries, hulled and quartered

4 cups blueberries

6 kiwis, peeled and cut into rounds

2 tangerines, peeled and cut into rounds

1 cup apricot preserves

2 (10-inch) store-bought graham
  cracker piecrusts

In a medium bowl, whisk together the milk, flour, granulated sugar, egg yolks, lemon zest, and vanilla until well blended. Transfer the mixture to a small saucepot and whisk slowly over medium heat until the custard thickens. Remove from the heat and refrigerate for 2 to 3 hours.

In a large bowl, toss the fruit and preserves to combine.

Divide the custard evenly between the piecrusts, then layer the fresh fruit on top. Serve immediately or refrigerate overnight.

ZEPPOLE

MAKES 16 SMALL ZEPPOLE

At the Jersey Shore in the summertime, the longest lines on the boardwalk are for the zeppole, or fried balls of dough. Same thing when the San Gennaro Feast—or just The Feast—rolls around. For good reason too—they're delicious. If we wanted zeppole and it wasn't summertime or The Feast, we'd go over to Pizza Town, which was famous for their zeppole, fried calzones, and slices. It used to be called Pizza Clown and had what looked like a giant red, white, and blue circus tent over it, but when the mini golf next door shut down, they changed it to Pizza Town. Before Basille's, it was the most popular place for pizza in Staten Island. Rodney Dangerfield even filmed a scene there for Easy Money. When we opened the restaurant, though, we started makin' our own zeppole from the leftover pizza dough. Pizza Town used a special dough for theirs, but for us, if we were in the mood for dessert, we just used what we had on hand. We'd let it proof to death with flour, salt, and yeast and then deep-fry it until it was crispy and golden brown on the outside but soft and cake-like in the middle. We loved zeppole so much that we even opened a dessert shop in 2009 called Led Zeppole.

1 cup all-purpose flour

1 teaspoon baking powder

2 teaspoons granulated sugar

½ teaspoon vanilla extract

4 cups vegetable oil

½ cup confectioners' sugar

In a large bowl, whisk together the flour, baking powder, granulated sugar, vanilla, and ½ cup water. Whisk until the consistency is even and sticky.

In a deep-fryer or a deep frying pan, heat the oil until it registers about 375°F on a deep-frying thermometer.

Scoop tablespoons of the batter into the hot oil and cook for 4 minutes, or until browned on all sides. Transfer the zeppole to a paper towel.

Put the cooked zeppole in a paper bag with the confectioners' sugar, seal the bag, and shake vigorously for 30 seconds. Remove and enjoy!

CANNOLI

MAKES 8 CANNOLI

Our great-grandfather made cannoli in the bakery, so when he had the shops, these would always be on the table for the holidays like Christmas and Easter. After that, Fran's dad made them in a bakery he owned for a short time on Long Island. Fran remembers goin' out there with his sister and her eating like eight cannoli, then throwin' up in the sink in the back of the store. After that shop closed, we got our cannoli from Alfonso's in Staten Island or from Court Pastry.

The thing is, though, they aren't too bad to make yourself now that they sell pretty good cannoli shells at the store. It beats having to make the shells, because everything's gotta be just right or it all falls apart. The filling, on the other hand, is so easy. You just gotta buy the ricotta impastata, *which is ricotta that's been dried out in the oven so it's very dry and spreads like cream cheese. Then you add some mascarpone cheese, a little rum, a little vanilla, and a little sugar. And once you've filled your cannoli, you can use the leftover filling in all different ways— stuff zeppole with it, fill cakes with it, put it on toast, put it on a bagel, or eat it right outta the bowl.*

If you do end up buyin' cannoli from a store instead, just make sure they haven't been sittin' in the case all day, gettin' soggy on the bottom. A good shop will either be turning them over fast or fillin' 'em for you fresh.

If you can't find ricotta impastata, *use mascarpone instead. Or wrap some regular ricotta in cheesecloth, set it in a strainer over a bowl, and leave it in the refrigerator overnight so all the liquid drains out.*

1 cup *ricotta impastata*
  or additional mascarpone

1 cup mascarpone cheese

½ cup confectioners' sugar

1 teaspoon vanilla extract

2 tablespoons lemon zest

½ teaspoon ground cinnamon

8 store-bought cannoli shells

In a medium bowl, combine the *ricotta impastata*, mascarpone, sugar, vanilla, lemon zest, and cinnamon and stir until smooth. Cover and refrigerate overnight.

To fill the cannoli, spoon the filling into a pastry bag fitted with a plain tip. Pipe the filling in one end of the cannoli shell so it fills halfway. Then fill it completely from the other end.

DESSERT DESSERT

At holidays and special occasions, there was one more course after the dessert pastries. It was a spread of nuts, fruit (fresh and dried), and coffee (American and Italian). We called it "dessert dessert." When our grandma was putting out the assortment, Fran would always say, "Grandma, don't go nuts." She'd call him a wiseass.

There aren't any rules when it comes to dessert dessert; just put out what you like. For us, it was usually mixed nuts, dried fruit like apricots and dates, candied mango and pineapple, fresh pears, oranges, bananas, grapes—a lot of grapes—and walnuts and chestnuts—always walnuts and chestnuts. If Sal's family was there, there'd be figs, too, because after they moved out to the country, they had fig trees. As for coffee, there was always the two kinds, because not everybody liked espresso. Either way, the adults called their black coffee "demitasse." Our grandma would make it in a little old-fashioned coffeepot on the stove and serve it with Sambuca, anisette, Tia Maria, or Frangelico.

ACKNOWLEDGMENTS

WE'D LIKE TO THANK:

Our mothers, Joy Garcia and Bella Basille

Our fathers, Frankie Garcia and Vito Basille

Our siblings, Vinny, Vinny, Dominick, Aimee, Maria, and Kaitlin

Brandon R. Linker

Rachel Holtzman

Janis Donnaud

Karen Murgolo

Quentin Bacon

Jessica Weiner

Gary Tooth

Jose Neri

Uncle Tommy

Uncle Sal Basille

Aunt Loulou

Uncle Greg

And all of the Basille's, Solo Bella, Solo Tu, and
Artichoke staff, past and present.

INDEX

ABOUT THE AUTHORS

First cousins and best friends Francis Garcia and Sal Basille opened Artichoke Basille's on Fourteenth Street in 2008 after leaving their parents' thriving restaurant business in Staten Island. They immediately scored glowing reviews in the *New York Times*, *New York Post*, and *New York Magazine*. David Chang, Keith Richards, Leonardo DiCaprio, Drew Barrymore, and Martin Scorsese are all fans.

They've since expanded Artichoke to six locations in New York City and Berkeley, California. In 2011, they launched a frozen pizza line, and they appear on the Cooking Channel's series *Pizza Masters*, which features Sal and Fran visiting the best pizzerias in the country.

Rachel Holtzman is a writer who lives in Chicago with her husband, son, and two pugs.